Cookie Doughlicious

COOKIE DOUGHLICIOUS

50 Cookie Dough Recipes for Candies, Cakes, *and* More

LARA FERRONI

RUNNING PRESS
PHILADELPHIA · LONDON

Books published by Running Press are available at special
discounts for bulk purchases in the United States by
corporations, institutions, and other organizations. For more
information, please contact the Special Markets Department
at the Perseus Books Group, 2300 Chestnut Street, Suite
200, Philadelphia, PA 19103, or call (800) 810-4145, ext.
5000, or e-mail special.markets@perseusbooks.com.

ISBN 978-0-7624-4538-7
Library of Congress Control Number: 2013945769

E-book ISBN 978-0-7624-5176-0

9 8 7 6 5 4 3 2 1
Digit on the right indicates the number of this printing

Cover and interior design by Ashley Haag
Edited by Jordana Tusman
Typography: Willow, Fairplex, and Abadi

Running Press Book Publishers
2300 Chestnut Street
Philadelphia, PA 19103-4371

Visit us on the web!
www.offthemenublog.com

CONTENTS

REALLY WILD STUFF   115

INTRODUCTION

Who hasn't given in to a guilty spoonful (or five) of cookie dough straight from the bowl? There's just something irresistible about the ooey-gooey sweet softness of cookie dough that hasn't yet been baked into a crispy, crunchy golden round. Maybe it's the simple creamy mixture of sugar and butter that is so appealing, or maybe it's because it was always off-limits. Whatever the reason, cookie dough is so tempting that it has made its way into everything from ice cream to energy bars.

Still, when the opportunity of writing a whole book on cookie dough was in front of me, I was skeptical. Sure, everyone loves cookie dough, but is there really enough to write a whole book about it? So I sat down and made myself a list to test out what I might write about and quickly came up with a list of recipes that had me running to the kitchen, eager to bake. I took a few of my newly created concoctions to friends and neighbors, and their eyes lit up asking for more—I knew I had a cookbook to write.

First, I had to figure out how to make the dough less risky to eat raw. What your mother always told you was right: Most raw cookie doughs that contain eggs have some risk of making you sick, even if it is small. Chances are, it won't happen to you, but if it does, it won't be something you quickly forget. So, I'll show you that you can eat the cookie dough with these safe to eat, egg-free dough recipes that taste just like the dough you can bake.

Then I thought, why limit it to chocolate chip? What about all the other amazing flavors of cookie dough? From rich chocolate hazelnut to boozy rum raisin to sophisticated pistachio-lemon, or your childhood favorites, such as chocolate wafers, peanut butter, and gingerbread, the list of deliciousness goes on and on, with twenty different cookie dough flavors in total, featuring chocolate, sugar, spice, nuts, and fruit doughs, all tempting to eat straight from the bowl.

Once you've had your fill from the bowl, you can take your indulgence beyond the spoon and turn your favorite cookie dough into one of over fifty impossible-to-resist candies, cakes, frozen treats, and some really wild recipes that you might never expect. I've picked out my favorite flavor combinations for everything from a cookie dough tarte tatin to ice-cream sandwiches to homemade fudge. Some of the recipes are fancier than others, but all are mouthwatering.

Deep-fried chocolate chip cookie dough, anyone? Did someone say chocolate espresso cookie dough tiramisu? Are peanut butter cookie dough–stuffed pretzels calling your name? How about pumpkin cookie dough waffles? Or pick your favorite flavor of dough and mix and match to create entirely new and amazing cookie dough concoctions. The world is your cookie dough bowl!

Or did I have you at "spoonful?"

INGREDIENTS

You'll have the best-tasting cookie dough if you use the best-quality ingredients, but for the most part, you should be able to use whatever you normally buy. Here are a few recommendations based on how I typically stock my kitchen.

Butter

These recipes were developed using unsalted butter, so the salt is added in the recipe if needed. If you prefer to use salted butter, just reduce the salt appropriately in the recipe. Butter should be at room temperature to ensure the creamiest cookie dough results. If you only have cold butter, try a cheese grater to break it into small chunks, and it will soften up quickly.

Chocolate

For recipes that call for chocolate, I typically use semisweet, but bittersweet or milk chocolate in your favorite brand are fine to substitute as well. For the right way to melt chocolate without scorching, see "double boiler" on page xiv.

Cocoa Powder

The recipes in this book call for unsweetened natural cocoa powder, except in the Chocolate Wafer Cookie Dough (page 5) and in the Sugar Cookie Dough Sandwich Cookies (page 61), where Dutch-processed cocoa will produce a darker (and more Oreo-like) cookie. You can usually find Dutch-processed cocoa powder right next to the natural cocoa powder or in with the bulk foods. If you can't find it, using natural cocoa powder, one for one, is fine; the cookie dough will just be a bit lighter in flavor and color.

Eggs

Although none of the dough recipes in this book contain eggs, many of the dessert recipes in the book still call for them. Use fresh, large eggs wherever eggs are needed.

Flour

Unless specified, these recipes were designed with organic all-purpose flour. I try to buy locally produced flour, but I also like King Arthur and Bob's Red Mill organic flours. It's important to use a high-quality flour that you trust, as flour has been known to contain *E. coli*. That bacteria wouldn't be squashed through the normal baking process in uncooked cookie dough so even though it's a remote chance, it's not one you want to mess with.

Instead, you can kick that *E. coli's* butt by cooking your flour first. Yeah, it's kind of weird, but better safe than sorry, right? I mean, you're leaving out the eggs so you are safe; what's a couple of minutes to bake some flour?

Here's what you do: Place your flour in a microwave-safe bowl, and cook on full power for 2 minutes, stopping, removing the bowl, and stirring with a fork every 20 seconds. When done, sift the flour to pull out any clumps that have formed.

Fine Print: You, like me, probably don't have sophisticated bacteria-measuring equipment in your kitchen, so I can't guarantee that your cooked flour will be completely bacteria-free. Proceed at your own discretion.

The cookie doughs in this book can also be made gluten-free, with a non-bean-based gluten-free flour mix, such as Cup4Cup, or your own favorite homemade version. Although the finished recipes haven't been tested with gluten-free flours, most should work with a one-to-one substitution.

Milk and Cream

Feel free to use any fat content that you prefer for milk, unless a certain kind is specified in the recipe. I typically use organic 2% milk, but whole milk and fat-free will also work. Where cream is called for, use heavy whipping cream with a fat content of 36 to 40 percent.

Nuts

Use fresh, good-quality nuts, as old nuts can go rancid and have an off flavor. It's particularly important to use good-quality pistachios that are roasted in the shell instead of out. Not only will they be a more beautiful vivid green, they'll also have a more complex flavor. Specialty Middle Eastern or Mediterranean markets are most likely to have the best options. Bazzini Ram's Head pistachios are good ones if you can find them.

Salt

Sea, kosher, or table—use what you like! I typically use fine-grain kosher salt, except for a few recipes where a flakier or coarser grain is needed and specifically called for.

Sugar

For the smoothest cookie dough, I recommend using superfine sugar rather than standard granulated. Either will do, but you may need to cream your sugar and butter a bit longer to avoid a slightly crunchy dough. If you don't have superfine sugar on hand, you can make your own by pulsing standard granulated sugar in a food processor for about 1 minute.

For brown sugar, light or dark are fine unless otherwise specified, but make sure you get the soft-moist type of brown sugar rather than brown raw sugar, which will give your cookie dough a gritty quality.

A few of the recipes (such as the cookie dough pops) call for working with hot sugar. Molten sugar is remarkably hotter than you might think, so never, ever touch it with your skin! Especially not your tongue!

TOOLS

It's worth investing in a few tools to make your baking a breeze. Here is a list of the tools that are handy to have at your fingertips when cooking from this book.

Baking pans

If you don't have quite the size baking pan the recipe calls for, you may need to adjust your quantities or baking times. If your pan is smaller, be sure to check for doneness at least 5 minutes before the specified time in the recipe. If larger, check at the indicated time.

Baking sheets

I prefer to line baking sheets with parchment paper. It makes it a breeze to quickly remove whatever you are baking from the sheet, and cleanup is as easy as tossing the parchment paper into the trash.

Blender

My immersion blender is my favorite kitchen gadget. Not only is it inexpensive, but it quickly purées everything from soup to nuts, and is my go-to tool for shakes. A stand blender is a fine substitute if you don't have one.

Double boiler

A few of the recipes in this book call for melted chocolate. As chocolate needs to be melted gently so it doesn't scorch, it's best to use a double boiler, or a metal or glass bowl sitting over a pot of boiling water to heat slowly. You can also melt chocolate in a microwave, stopping to stir every 5 to 10 seconds to ensure the chocolate melts without burning.

Food processor

There are a few recipes that need a food processor. Any size will do (I use the smaller size), but you really will be happier using one. If you want, you can use a mixer for the Chocolate Wafer Cookie Dough (page 5), Sugar Cookie Dough Sandwich Cookies (page 59), and Butterscotch Cookie Dough Nanaimo Bars (page 67). For the energy bars (page 73), use a blender to purée the mixture, but be sure not to overblend.

Instant-read thermometer

A good instant-read thermometer is incredibly helpful to have on hand to make sure oil temperature is in the right zone when frying, but even more crucial to get the molten sugar to just the right stage when making the Chocolate Cookie Dough "Cooksie" Pops (page 83). You don't need to spend a lot of money on one, though. The $15 Taylor thermometers work just as well as the fancy digital variety.

Mixer

I use a stand mixer to make the cookie doughs (as well as for the finished recipes), but a hand mixer or even a spoon or whisk with a bit of arm muscle are just fine for making the cookie dough and recipes in this book.

Utensils

Beyond typical baking tools, such as measuring spoons and cups, a good rubber spatula, and a whisk, it's handy to also have a small (1-inch) ice-cream scoop or melon baller when you're working with dough.

WORKING *with* COOKIE DOUGH

The cookie dough recipes in this book all create a soft cookie dough that should be easy to roll into a ball. If the dough is too crumbly, or you need a consistency more like a frosting for the recipe you are working with, you can mix in a small splash of milk or water. If the dough seems too moist, don't be tempted to add more flour. Instead, cover and chill the dough for just a few minutes and it will firm up.

You can store prepared cookie dough in an airtight container for up to 5 days, but you'll want to bring it close to room temperature when it's time to use it, so the butter can soften. Only the brownie dough is best used the same day that

you make it, as the chocolate will harden significantly when chilled and will stay firm even at room temperature. If needed, you can microwave the raw cookie dough for about 10 seconds to soften it, but be careful not to overheat it.

What happens if you bake it? Well, not much good for most of the doughs. Without eggs and leavening, you'll have pretty flat cookies that are more crumbly than you'd probably want to eat. You can, however, bake the peanut butter cookie dough if you are so inclined! Just bake slightly flattened chilled dough balls for about 12 minutes at 350°F.

THE COOKIE DOUGHS

Here's where you start, and perhaps finish, if all you are looking for is a quick raw cookie dough hit. You'll find all the cookie dough recipes in this chapter, grouped by flavor: Chunkful of Chocolate (page 2), Sugar and Spice (page 10), Nutter Batter (page 15), and Fruit and Cereal (page 21). Each of the cookie dough recipes make about 1 cup of dough, give or take a few spoonfuls, and are all quite easy to double as needed for a larger batch.

CHUNKFUL *of* CHOCOLATE

Cookie dough has become practically synonymous with chocolate chip cookie dough, and it's not surprising since this dough is the quintessential flavor combination of sweet with just a hint of salty and plenty of chocolaty goodness. If you like chocolate chip cookie dough, you may find some of these doughs, such as Rocky Road (page 8) or Brownie (page 6), even harder to resist.

Chocolate Chip Cookie Dough

4 tablespoons (½ stick) unsalted butter, at room temperature
2 tablespoons granulated sugar
2 tablespoons packed light or dark brown sugar
½ teaspoon vanilla extract
1 tablespoon milk
½ cup all-purpose flour
¼ teaspoon salt
2 ounces (¼ cup) chocolate chips

In a medium bowl, beat the butter and sugars for 3 minutes, or until well creamed. Stir in the vanilla and milk. Add the flour and salt and mix, by hand or on low speed with an electric mixer, until well blended. Stir in the chocolate chips. Mix well.

TIP! *Want double chocolate chip dough? Add ¼ cup of sifted unsweetened natural cocoa powder along with the flour.*

This dough is used in Chocolate Chip Cookie Dough Crispy Rice Treats (page 79), Chocolate Chip Cookie Dough Dip or Spread (page 145), and Deep-Fried Chocolate Chip Cookie Dough (page 121).

Chocolate Espresso Cookie Dough

4 tablespoons (½ stick) unsalted butter,
  at room temperature
2 tablespoons superfine sugar
2 tablespoons packed light or dark
  brown sugar
1 tablespoon brewed espresso, cooled
½ cup all-purpose flour
¼ cup unsweetened natural cocoa
  powder
¼ teaspoon salt

In a medium bowl, beat the butter and sugars for 3 minutes, or until well creamed. Stir in the espresso. Add the flour, cocoa powder, and salt and mix, by hand or on low speed with an electric mixer, until well blended.

This dough is used in Chocolate Espresso Cookie Dough Tiramisu (page 41) and Chocolate Espresso Cookie Dough Monkey Bread (page 129).

Chocolate Wafer Cookie Dough

¾ cup all-purpose flour

⅓ cup unsweetened Dutch-processed cocoa powder

½ cup light or dark brown sugar

Pinch of salt

6 tablespoons unsalted butter, at room temperature

1 tablespoon milk

1 teaspoon vanilla extract

Combine the flour, cocoa, sugar, and salt in the bowl of a food processor (or a stand mixer with the paddle attachment) and pulse several times to mix thoroughly. Drop in the butter by the tablespoon, and pulse to create a crumbly mixture. With the food processor running, drizzle in the milk and vanilla until the mixture starts to stick together to form a dough, about 1 minute.

TIP! *Want "thin mint" cookie dough? Add a couple of drops of peppermint extract to this dough!*

This dough is used in the Chocolate Cookie Dough "Cooksie" Pops (page 83) and Cookie Dough and Cream Ice Cream (page 93).

Brownie Cookie Dough

4 tablespoons (½ stick) unsalted butter,
    at room temperature
½ cup superfine sugar
1 teaspoon vanilla extract
4 ounces dark chocolate, melted (½ cup)
¼ cup milk
½ cup all-purpose flour
¼ cup unsweetened natural cocoa powder
Pinch of salt

In a medium bowl, beat the butter and sugar for 3 minutes, or until well creamed. Stir in the vanilla and melted chocolate. Slowly stream in the milk. Add the flour, cocoa powder, and salt and mix, by hand or on low speed with an electric mixer, until well blended.

TIP! *This dough hardens when chilled, so it's best when used immediately.*

This dough is used in the Brownie Cookie Dough Mud Pie (page 31) and Mocha Brownie Cookie Dough Shake (page 111).

Samoa Cookie Dough

4 tablespoons (½ stick) unsalted butter, at room temperature
¼ cup superfine sugar
¼ cup packed light or dark brown sugar
½ teaspoon vanilla extract
¼ cup all-purpose flour
½ teaspoon salt
½ cup unsweetened shredded coconut
2 ounces (¼ cup) chocolate chips
¼ cup caramel sauce

In a medium bowl, beat the butter and sugars for 3 minutes, or until well creamed. Stir in the vanilla. Add the flour and salt and mix, by hand or on low speed with an electric mixer, until well blended. Fold in the coconut and chocolate chips. Then swirl in the caramel sauce by gently folding, being careful not to overstir.

This dough is used in the Samoa Cookie Dough Energy Bars (page 73), Samoa Cookie Dough Coconut Ice Cream (page 98), and Samoa Cookie Dough Egg Rolls (page 118).

Rocky Road Cookie Dough

4 tablespoons (½ stick) unsalted butter,
    at room temperature
2 tablespoons superfine sugar
2 tablespoons packed light or dark brown
    sugar
½ teaspoon vanilla extract
⅓ cup all-purpose flour
¼ cup unsweetened natural cocoa
    powder
¼ teaspoon salt
¼ cup mini marshmallows
¼ cup toasted walnuts or pecans,
    coarsely chopped
¼ cup chocolate chips

In a medium bowl, beat the butter and sugars for 3 minutes, or until well creamed. Stir in the vanilla. Add the flour, cocoa powder, and salt and mix, by hand or on low speed with an electric mixer, until well blended. Stir in the marshmallows, nuts, and chocolate chips. Mix well.

This dough is used in the Rocky Road Cookie Dough Molten Chocolate Cake (page 34) and Rocky Road Cookie Dough Fudge (page 74).

Chocolate Cherry Cookie Dough

4 tablespoons (½ stick) unsalted butter,
  at room temperature
2 tablespoons superfine sugar
2 tablespoons packed light or dark brown
  sugar
½ teaspoon vanilla extract
½ cup all-purpose flour
¼ cup unsweetened natural cocoa
  powder
¼ teaspoon salt
½ cup dried cherries, coarsely chopped

In a medium bowl, beat the butter and sugars for 3 minutes, or until well creamed. Stir in the vanilla. Add the flour, cocoa powder, and salt and mix, by hand or on low speed with an electric mixer, until well blended. Stir in the cherries and mix well.

This dough is used for the Chocolate Cherry Cookie Dough–Filled Cupcakes (page 29) and Chocolate Cherry Cookie Dough Parfait (page 107).

SUGAR *and* SPICE

It's amazing the different flavors you can get from sugar, butter, and a pinch or two of spice. These doughs may have the same basic components but certainly don't taste the same. One thing they all have in common: They're delicious!

Sugar Cookie Dough

4 tablespoons (½ stick) unsalted butter, at room temperature
¼ cup superfine sugar
½ teaspoon vanilla extract
½ cup all-purpose flour
¼ teaspoon salt

In a medium bowl, beat the butter and sugar for 3 minutes, or until well creamed. Stir in the vanilla. Add the flour and salt and mix, by hand or on low speed with an electric mixer, until well blended.

This dough is used in Sugar Cookie Dough Sandwich Cookies (page 59), Sugar Cookie Dough Truffles (page 87), and Baked Sugar Cookie Dough–Stuffed Apples (page 139).

Snickerdoodle Cookie Dough

4 tablespoons (½ stick) unsalted butter, at room temperature
¼ cup superfine sugar
½ teaspoon vanilla extract
1 tablespoon milk
½ cup all-purpose flour
½ teaspoon salt
½ teaspoon ground cinnamon, divided

In a medium bowl, beat the butter and sugar for 3 minutes, or until well creamed. Stir in the vanilla and milk. Add the flour, salt, and ¼ teaspoon of the cinnamon and mix, by hand or on low speed with an electric mixer, until well blended. Sprinkle the remaining cinnamon over the top of the dough, and fold it in, leaving some cinnamon streaks.

This dough is used in Snickerdoodle Cookie Dough Crisp (page 54), Snickerdoodle Cookie Dough Ice Pops (page 103), and Snickerdoodle Cookie Dough Cinnamon Rolls (page 133).

Butterscotch Cookie Dough

4 tablespoons (½ stick) unsalted butter, at room temperature, divided
¼ cup packed light or dark brown sugar
½ teaspoon vanilla extract
1 teaspoon bourbon or other whiskey (optional)
⅓ cup all-purpose flour
½ teaspoon salt
2 ounces (¼ cup) butterscotch chips (optional)

Heat 2 tablespoons of the butter in a heavy-bottomed skillet. It will foam, then settle, and then turn a lovely tan with the milk solids settling at the bottom. When the milk solids reach a golden caramel color, remove the pan from the heat. Stir in the remaining 2 tablespoons of butter so it melts and cools slightly.

In a medium bowl, beat the browned butter and sugar for 3 minutes, or until well creamed. Stir in the vanilla and bourbon. Add the flour and salt and mix, by hand or on low speed with an electric mixer, until well blended. Mix in the butterscotch chips, if you are using them.

This dough is used in Butterscotch Cookie Dough Nanaimo Bars (page 67) and Butterscotch Cookie Dough Ice-Cream Sandwiches (page 95).

Gingerbread Cookie Dough

4 tablespoons (½ stick) unsalted butter,
    at room temperature
¼ cup packed light or dark brown sugar
1 tablespoon unsulfured molasses
½ teaspoon vanilla extract
1 tablespoon milk
½ cup all-purpose flour
¼ teaspoon salt
¼ teaspoon ground ginger
¼ teaspoon ground allspice
⅛ teaspoon ground cinnamon
⅛ teaspoon ground cloves

In a medium bowl, beat the butter, sugar, and molasses for 3 minutes, or until well creamed. Stir in the vanilla and milk. Add the flour, salt, and all the spices and mix, by hand or on low speed with an electric mixer, until well blended.

This dough is used in the Dark Chocolate Gingerbread Cookie Dough Bonbons (page 69) and Gingerbread Cookie Dough "Crème" Brûlée (page 144).

NUTTER BATTER

Raw nutty dough is a bit of a conundrum. Raw nuts are really not nuts at their best. They can be bitter and mealy, and need to be heated to bring out their buttery goodness. On the flip side, nut-based cookies can quickly go from luscious to dry and brittle. The solution: toast the nuts, not the dough!

Peanut Butter Cookie Dough

4 tablespoons (½ stick) unsalted butter,
    at room temperature
2 tablespoons superfine sugar
2 tablespoons packed light or dark
    brown sugar
½ teaspoon vanilla extract
¼ cup smooth or chunky peanut butter
½ cup all-purpose flour
½ teaspoon salt
¼ cup dry-roasted, salted peanuts,
    chopped (optional)

In a medium bowl, beat the butter and sugars for 3 minutes, or until well creamed. Stir in the vanilla and peanut butter. Add the flour and salt and mix, by hand or on low speed with an electric mixer, until well blended. Stir in the chopped peanuts, if using, and mix well.

This dough is used in the Chocolate and Peanut Butter Cookie Dough Buckeyes (page 77), Peanut Butter Cookie Dough Fluffernutter (page 117), and Peanut Butter Cookie Dough–Stuffed Pretzels (page 141).

Chocolate Hazelnut Cookie Dough

4 tablespoons (½ stick) unsalted butter, at room temperature

4 tablespoons packed light or dark brown sugar

2 tablespoons superfine sugar

¼ cup store-bought or home-ground hazelnut butter

½ teaspoon vanilla extract

1 tablespoon milk

¼ cup all-purpose flour

2 tablespoons unsweetened natural cocoa powder

¼ teaspoon salt

In a medium bowl, beat the butter, sugars, and hazelnut butter for 3 minutes, or until well creamed. Stir in the vanilla and milk. Add the flour, cocoa powder, and salt and mix, by hand or on low speed with an electric mixer, until well blended.

TIP! *You can also easily sub ½ cup of chocolate hazelnut spread (such as Nutella) in place of the hazelnut butter, cocoa powder, and 2 tablespoons of the brown sugar.*

This dough is used in Chocolate Hazelnut Cookie Dough Toaster Tarts (page 46) and Chocolate Hazelnut Cookie Dough Profiteroles (page 149).

Cashew Caramel Cookie Dough

4 tablespoons (½ stick) unsalted butter, at room temperature
2 tablespoons granulated sugar
2 tablespoons packed light or dark brown sugar
½ teaspoon vanilla extract
1 tablespoon milk
½ cup all-purpose flour
¼ teaspoon salt
¼ cup salted cashews, roasted and chopped
3 ounces caramel sauce, slightly warmed

In a medium bowl, beat the butter and sugars for 3 minutes, or until well creamed. Stir in the vanilla and milk. Add the flour and salt and mix, by hand or on low speed with an electric mixer, until well blended. Mix in the chopped cashews and swirl in the caramel sauce. (The caramel sauce will pour better if it is just slightly warmed.)

TIP! *Want your cookie dough even nuttier?*
Add ¼ cup of cashew butter to the mixture.

This dough is used in the Cashew Caramel Cookie Dough Candy Bar (page 81), Cashew Caramel Cookie Dough Chocolate Ice Cream (page 112), and Cashew Caramel Cookie Dough Flautas (page 123).

Coconut Macaroon Cookie Dough

½ cup sweetened condensed milk
1 tablespoon all-purpose flour
¼ teaspoon salt
½ teaspoon vanilla extract
1 cup unsweetened shredded coconut

Place the sweetened condensed milk in a heavy-bottomed pot over medium heat. Add the flour and salt, and whisk thoroughly. Heat the mixture to a full boil, and continue to boil for about 2 minutes, or until it has thickened. Remove from the heat and whisk in the vanilla and coconut, and allow to cool before using.

This dough is used in the Coconut Macaroon Cookie Dough Tea Cakes (page 38) and Coconut Macaroon Cookie Dough Sundae (page 108).

Pecan Sandie Cookie Dough

4 tablespoons (½ stick) unsalted butter, at room temperature
¼ cup turbinado sugar
½ teaspoon vanilla extract
½ cup all-purpose flour
½ teaspoon salt
⅓ cup finely chopped pecans, toasted

In a medium bowl, beat the butter and sugar for 3 minutes, or until well creamed. (It will still be a bit "crunchy.") Stir in the vanilla. Add the flour and salt and mix, by hand or on low speed with an electric mixer, until well blended. Stir in the pecans and mix well.

This dough is used in the Pecan Sandie Cookie Dough Nut Log (page 147).

FRUIT *and* CEREAL

I'll admit it. I have unwittingly bitten into an oatmeal raisin cookie and felt the rush of disappointment that it wasn't chocolate chip. But then, I take another nibble, and another, and soon I'm completely smitten. I think you will be, too, with these fruit- and cereal-based cookie doughs.

Oatmeal Raisin Cookie Dough

4 tablespoons (½ stick) unsalted butter,
    at room temperature
¼ cup packed light or dark brown sugar
½ teaspoon vanilla extract
⅓ cup all-purpose flour
¼ teaspoon salt
¼ teaspoon ground cinnamon
¼ teaspoon ground allspice
⅓ cup rolled oats
¼ cup raisins, coarsely chopped

In a medium bowl, beat the butter and sugar for 3 minutes, or until well creamed. Stir in the vanilla. Add the flour, salt, and the spices and mix, by hand or on low speed with an electric mixer, until well blended. Stir in the oats and raisins and mix well.

TIP! *For yummy, boozy rum raisin cookie dough, just add 2 tablespoons of your favorite dark rum!*

This dough is used in the Oatmeal Raisin Cookie Dough Tarte Tatin (page 51), Oatmeal Raisin Cookie Dough Thick Shake (page 109), and Oatmeal Cookie Dough Porridge (page 132).

Cranberry Apple Cookie Dough

¼ cup dried cranberries, coarsely chopped

¼ cup dried apples, coarsely chopped

4 tablespoons (½ stick) unsalted butter,
    at room temperature

¼ cup superfine sugar

½ teaspoon vanilla extract

½ cup all-purpose flour

½ teaspoon salt

¼ cup rolled oats (optional)

In a bowl, soak the chopped cranberries and apples in hot water for about 15 minutes. Drain and set aside.

In a medium bowl, beat the butter and sugar for 3 minutes, or until well creamed. Stir in the vanilla. Add the flour and salt and mix, by hand or on low speed with an electric mixer, until well blended. Stir in the drained cranberries and apples and mix well. Stir in the rolled oats, if using, and mix well.

TIP! *This dough is also fantastic with dried apricots instead of the apples!*

This dough is used in the Cranberry Apple Cookie Dough Mini Pies (page 43), Yogurt-Covered Cranberry Apple Cookie Dough Pops (page 88), and Cranberry Apple Cookie Dough Aebleskivers (page 127).

Pumpkin Cookie Dough

4 tablespoons (½ stick) unsalted butter,
   at room temperature
¼ cup packed light or dark brown sugar
¼ cup pumpkin purée (not pumpkin
   pie filling)
1 teaspoon vanilla extract
1 teaspoon pure maple syrup
½ cup all-purpose flour
¼ teaspoon salt
¼ teaspoon ground cinnamon
¼ teaspoon ground nutmeg
¼ teaspoon ground ginger
¼ cup toasted pecans, coarsely chopped
   (optional)

In a medium bowl, beat the butter, sugar, and pumpkin purée for 3 minutes, or until well creamed. Stir in the vanilla and maple syrup. Add the flour, salt, and spices and mix, by hand or on low speed with an electric mixer, until well blended. Stir in the pecans, if using, and mix well.

This dough is used in the Pumpkin Cookie Dough Turnovers (page 49), Pumpkin Cookie Dough Thumbprint Cookies (page 64), Pumpkin Cookie Dough Ice Cream (page 105), and Pumpkin Cookie Dough Waffles (page 136).

Pistachio-Lemon Cookie Dough

6 tablespoons unsalted butter, at room temperature

¾ cup confectioners' sugar

2 teaspoons freshly squeezed lemon juice

Zest from ½ lemon

½ cup all-purpose flour

Pinch of salt

⅓ cup roasted, salted pistachios, finely chopped

In a medium bowl, beat the butter and sugar for 3 minutes, or until well creamed. Stir in the lemon juice and zest. Add the flour and salt and mix, by hand or on low speed with an electric mixer, until well blended. Stir in the pistachios and mix well.

This dough is used in the Pistachio-Lemon Cookie Dough Cheesecake (page 37), Pistachio-Lemon Cookie Dough–Filled Macarons (page 61), and Pistachio-Lemon Cookie Dough Sorbet (page 101).

CAKES, PIES, &TARTS

You get a lot of weird looks when you tell someone you are writing a cookbook on raw cookie dough. I answer with a few simple words: "Chocolate Espresso Cookie Dough Tiramisu. Rocky Road Cookie Dough Molten Chocolate Cake. Chocolate Hazelnut Cookie Dough Toaster Tarts. And that's just the cakes, pies, and tarts chapter." Then I hand them a napkin to wipe away the drool.

Chocolate Cherry Cookie Dough—Filled Cupcakes

Rich chocolate cupcakes, dark cherry cookie dough filling, cherry ganache glaze, and a vanilla frosting flower. Fancy, fancy. But not so fancy that you shouldn't smash one into your mouth as soon as possible.

MAKES 12 CUPCAKES

For the cupcakes:

6 tablespoons unsalted butter, at room
   temperature
1 cup granulated sugar
1 large egg
1 cup all-purpose flour
½ teaspoon baking soda
¼ teaspoon salt
⅓ cup unsweetened natural cocoa powder
1 cup milk
1 teaspoon vanilla extract

For the ganache:

6 ounces semisweet chocolate, chopped
½ cup heavy whipping cream
2 tablespoons cherry juice

½ cup Chocolate Cherry Cookie Dough
   (page 9)
1 ½ cups vanilla frosting (optional)

For the cupcakes:

Preheat the oven to 350°F. Line a 12-cup cupcake pan with cupcake liners.

In a bowl, beat the butter and sugar for 3 minutes, or until well creamed. Add the egg and beat until smooth.

Sift the flour, baking soda, salt, and cocoa powder into one bowl, and put the milk and vanilla into another.

Spoon about one third of the flour mixture into the butter mixture, and stir for about 1 minute. Add half of the milk mixture, and stir to combine. Spoon in another third of the flour mixture, mixing to combine, followed by the milk mixture, and finishing with the rest of the flour.

Spoon the batter into the cupcake liners (an ice-cream scoop makes this a breeze!), and fill each about three quarters full. Bake for about 25 minutes, or until a toothpick inserted into the middle of the cupcake comes out clean. Let the cupcakes cool on a wire rack, still in the tin, until completely cool.

For the ganache:

Place the chocolate in a medium bowl. Combine the cream and cherry juice in a saucepan over medium-low heat just until it begins to simmer (do not boil), and then pour over the chocolate. Let it sit for about 2 minutes, and then stir until smooth.

Once cool, cut a little cone from the top of the cupcake and fill with about 2 teaspoons of the softened cookie dough. Replace the cone (tearing off the tip as needed) of cake, and then spread the chocolate ganache over the top. Pipe on a little flower of the vanilla frosting, if using. Serve immediately.

TIP! *These cupcakes taste amazing with any of the chocolate cookie dough flavors (page 2).*

Brownie Cookie Dough Mud Pie

In the world of over-the-top desserts, this one has to rank in the upper echelons: chocolate crusted brownie pecan pie with frosting. And, if that's not enough for you, there's always the billow of whipped cream and hearty drizzle of chocolate syrup on top.

MAKES 6 TO 8 SERVINGS

1 ¼ cups plus 2 tablespoons all-purpose flour, divided

¼ cup unsweetened natural cocoa powder

2 tablespoons granulated sugar

1 ¼ teaspoons salt, divided

6 tablespoons unsalted butter, chilled, plus ½ cup (1 stick) unsalted butter, at room temperature

1 teaspoon freshly squeezed lemon juice

½ cup ice water, divided

1 ½ cups pecan halves, toasted

4 ounces semisweet or bittersweet chocolate, coarsely chopped

¾ cup packed dark brown sugar

4 large eggs, at room temperature

½ cup light corn syrup

2 tablespoons dark molasses

2 teaspoons pure vanilla extract

½ cup Brownie Cookie Dough (page 6)

1 ounce cream cheese, at room temperature

2 tablespoons plain yogurt

Whipped cream, for garnish (optional)

Chocolate syrup, for garnish (optional)

. . . .

Whisk together 1 ¼ cups of the flour and the cocoa powder, granulated sugar, and 1 teaspoon of the salt. Work in the 6 tablespoons of chilled butter until the mixture resembles wet sand, with pea-size lumps of butter still visible. Add the lemon juice and 3 tablespoons of the ice water and mix with a fork until it is absorbed. Then add the remaining 5 tablespoons of ice water, tablespoon by tablespoon, just until you get a shaggy dough that starts to hang together. You most likely won't use all the water.

Shape the dough into a rough 4 x 6-inch rectangle, wrap in plastic wrap, and refrigerate for at least 30 minutes, or up to 2 days.

Preheat the oven to 400°F.

Place the chilled dough on a lightly floured work surface, and roll into a 10-inch circle. Place in a 9-inch glass pie plate, and prick all over with a fork. Cover with aluminum foil, fill with pie weights or dried beans, and bake for 20 minutes. Remove from the oven and let cool. Reduce the oven temperature to 350°F.

Toss the pecans, chocolate, and remaining 2 tablespoons of flour together and set aside.

Cream the ½ cup of butter and the brown sugar with an electric mixer on medium speed until light and fluffy, about 3 minutes. Add the eggs, 1 at a time, beating well after each addition and scraping down the sides of the bowl. Add the corn syrup, molasses, vanilla, and remaining ¼ teaspoon of salt and beat with a whisk attachment (or by hand with a whisk) until incorporated. Fold in the chocolate mixture.

Pour the mixture into the cooled pie shell and bake at 350°F until set, 45 minutes to an hour, or until a knife inserted into the middle comes out clean. Let cool completely on a wire rack.

Place the cookie dough, cream cheese, and yogurt in the bowl of a mixer, and stir to blend. Spread over the top of the cooled chocolate pie. Top with whipped cream, if you'd like, and then drizzle with chocolate syrup.

Rocky Road Cookie Dough Molten Chocolate Cake

Breaking news: Molten chocolate cake and cookie dough have now joined forces to create the world's greatest dessert. Marshmallows, chocolate, and nuts all played key roles in the negotiations.

MAKES 4 SMALL CAKES

½ cup Rocky Road Cookie Dough
  (page 8)
4 ounces bittersweet chocolate
4 tablespoons (½ stick) unsalted butter
2 large eggs
⅓ cup granulated sugar
¼ teaspoon salt
3 tablespoons all-purpose flour
Whipped cream, for garnish
About 12 raspberries, for garnish

Preheat the oven to 400°F.

Butter 4 (¾-cup) ramekins, and set aside.

Using a small scoop, such as a melon baller, make 4 little orbs of cookie dough, and place them on a waxed paper–lined baking sheet. Chill for 10 to 15 minutes in the freezer, or until firm.

In a heavy-bottomed pot over low heat, combine the chocolate and butter and stir until melted and smooth, about 3 minutes. Remove from the heat, and allow to cool for about 5 minutes.

In the bowl of a mixer, beat the eggs with the sugar and salt until light in color and smooth. Stream in the chocolate mixture, then stir in the flour. Pour the batter into the prepared ramekins, dividing the batter equally. Place a cookie dough ball in the center of each ramekin, and push down to cover it with the batter.

Bake for 10 to 12 minutes, or until the sides are set but the center is still soft. Serve immediately by inverting each ramekin onto a dessert plate. Garnish with a bit of whipped cream and fresh raspberries.

TIP! *Any of the chocolate cookie dough recipes (page 2) would be delicious in this molten chocolate cake.*

Pistachio-Lemon Cookie Dough Cheesecake

I could make my own graham cracker crust, but that feels like it flies in the face of this almost-no-work-but-freakishly-delicious cheesecake. So, instead, I use a store-bought crust, and bask in the extra 10 minutes I have in the day.

MAKES 8 HEARTY SLICES OF CHEESECAKE

1 (6-ounce) graham cracker crust
8 ounces cream cheese, at room
   temperature
1 cup Pistachio-Lemon Cookie Dough
   (page 25)
10 ounces sweetened condensed milk
¼ cup freshly squeezed lemon juice
1 teaspoon vanilla extract
Chopped pistachios, for garnish

Unwrap the graham cracker crust and place it in the freezer to chill while you make the filling.

Mix the cream cheese and cookie dough until smooth with an electric mixer on medium speed or with a spoon, and pour in the sweetened condensed milk, ¼ cup at a time, or until well combined. Beat in the lemon juice and vanilla.

Pour the filling into the chilled crust and sprinkle with some chopped pistachios. Cover with plastic wrap and freeze for an hour before serving to make it easier to slice. Once sliced, store in the refrigerator, covered, for up to 2 days.

Coconut Macaroon Cookie Dough Tea Cakes

Stir, spoon, bake, and frost. Now you have no excuse not to have a little treat with your tea!

½ cup (1 stick) unsalted butter

1 cup confectioners' sugar

⅔ cup whole wheat pastry flour

¼ teaspoon salt

½ cup blanched almonds, finely ground

4 large egg whites

½ teaspoon vanilla extract

1 cup Coconut Macaroon Cookie Dough (page 19)

2 tablespoons milk

½ cup chocolate chips, melted

Preheat the oven to 400°F. Generously butter 8 (3-inch-wide, 1-inch-deep) baking tins or muffin tin cups.

In a small skillet, heat the butter over medium heat until melted. Stir occasionally, and continue to heat until the milk solids turn golden brown.

Sift the sugar, flour, and salt together into the bowl of a stand mixer. Whisk in the ground almonds. Then slowly stir in the egg whites until moistened. Continue stirring, a tiny bit quicker, and add the browned butter and beat until smooth. Stir in the vanilla.

Spoon the batter into the prepared cups, filling halfway. Bake the cakes for about 15 minutes, or until the edges are golden brown. Allow the cakes to cool completely before removing from the tins.

Mix the cookie dough and milk until spreadable. Frost each cake with a generous dollop of the cookie dough. Drizzle a squiggly line of the melted chocolate chips over each cake.

Chocolate Espresso Cookie Dough Tiramisu

DON'T WORRY: The cookie dough doesn't weigh down this tiramisu! Whipped up with mascarpone and a bit of cream, it transforms into a fluffy chocolate espresso miracle.

½ cup brewed espresso, cooled

1 teaspoon granulated sugar

½ cup mascarpone

½ cup Chocolate Espresso Cookie Dough (page 4)

1 ½ cups heavy whipping cream, chilled, divided

2 tablespoons confectioners' sugar

8 ladyfinger cookies

Unsweetened cocoa powder, for dusting

Mix the espresso and sugar together in a small bowl and set aside.

In a medium bowl, whisk together the mascarpone, cookie dough, and ½ cup of the cream and set aside.

To make whipped cream, in a separate bowl, whisk the remaining cup of cream with the confectioners' sugar until soft peaks form.

Set 4 (4- to 5-ounce) dessert dishes or ramekins next to one another, and dollop a spoonful of the mascarpone mixture into the bottom of each. Break a ladyfinger in half and quickly dip each half in the espresso mixture, and place side by side in the dish. Top with a dollop of the mascarpone mixture and a dollop of whipped cream. Repeat with another ladyfinger, mascarpone, and a final layer of whipped cream.

Chill for about an hour and dust with cocoa powder before serving.

Cranberry Apple Cookie Dough Mini Pies

You've probably eaten a lot of pie in your life. But I bet you've never had pies like these itty-bitty cookie dough concoctions. Each pie is a wee bite of melty cookie dough dotted with cranberries and apples in just the right spots.

MAKES 12 MINI PIES

1 cup all-purpose flour
¼ cup plus 1 tablespoon granulated sugar
¼ teaspoon salt
4 tablespoons (½ stick) unsalted butter, chilled
6 tablespoons ice water
½ cup Cranberry Apple Cookie Dough (page 23)

Whisk together the flour, 1 tablespoon of the sugar, and the salt. Work in the butter until the mixture holds together when you squeeze it, with pecan-size lumps of butter still visible.

Add 3 tablespoons of the ice water and mix with a fork until it is absorbed. Then add 3 more tablespoons of ice water, tablespoon by tablespoon, just until you get a shaggy dough ball. You most likely won't use all the water.

Shape the dough into a rough 4-inch round, wrap in plastic wrap, and refrigerate for at least 30 minutes, or up to 2 days.

Preheat the oven to 350°F.

Place the chilled dough on a lightly floured work surface, and roll to about ¼ inch thick, about a 10 x 6-inch rectangle. Cut out 3-inch rounds with a cookie cutter or a large glass, rerolling the scraps as needed. Press each round into the cup of a muffin tin. It will just barely come up the sides of the tin. Bake for 15 minutes, or until the crust is golden brown all over. Remove the pie shells from the oven, and preheat the broiler.

Spoon the cookie dough into the pie shells and sprinkle each mini pie with a little bit of the remaining granulated sugar. Place the pies (still in the muffin tin) under the broiler until the sugar caramelizes, about 3 minutes. The pies are best served immediately but will keep in a pie keeper for several days.

TIP! *You can fill these little pie shells with any of the cookie dough flavors. Try the Chocolate Hazelnut Cookie Dough (page 17) or the Pumpkin Cookie Dough (page 24).*

Chocolate Hazelnut Cookie Dough Toaster Tarts

Oh, toaster tarts. Good morning to you. How I love your buttery crust, rich warm chocolate hazelnut cookie dough filling, and sheen of icing. You are the perfect way to start the day.

MAKES 8 TOASTER TARTS

2 cups all-purpose flour

2 tablespoons granulated sugar

Pinch of salt

½ cup (1 stick) unsalted butter, chilled

½ cup ice water

1 large egg

½ cup Chocolate Hazelnut Cookie Dough (page 17)

½ cup confectioners' sugar

1 tablespoon milk

Whisk together the flour, granulated sugar, and salt. Work in the butter until the mixture holds together when you squeeze it, with pecan-size lumps of butter still visible. Add 3 tablespoons of the ice water and mix with a fork until it is absorbed. Then add 5 tablespoons of the ice water, tablespoon by tablespoon, just until you get a shaggy dough ball. You most likely won't use all the water.

Shape the dough into a rough 4 x 6-inch rectangle, wrap in plastic wrap, and refrigerate for at least 30 minutes, or up to 2 days.

Place the chilled dough on a lightly floured work surface, and cut it into 4 equal pieces. Roll each piece into a rectangle about ⅛ inch thick. Trim off the edges to create 4 rectangles about 8 x 6 inches each. Cover the dough with plastic wrap. Beat the egg with 1 tablespoon of water, and brush it over 1 piece of the dough. Imagine the dough divided into quarters, and place a heaping tablespoon of cookie dough in the center of each quarter and gently spread, leaving a gap at the edges. Top with another rolled piece of dough, and press gently to seal around each of the pockets. Repeat with the remaining dough.

Carefully cut each piece into 3 x 4-inch quarters, and use a fork to pinch the edges. Place the tarts on a parchment-lined baking sheet, and cover with plastic wrap. Chill in the refrigerator for 30 minutes.

Preheat the oven to 350°F.

Brush the chilled tarts with the remaining egg wash, and using a fork, prick vent holes in the top of each tart.

Bake the tarts for 25 to 30 minutes, or until they are golden brown. Allow them to cool slightly before eating or icing.

To ice the tarts, mix together the confectioners' sugar with the milk and stir until smooth, adding a tiny bit more milk, if needed. Then spread all over the cooled tarts.

TIP! *These toaster tarts are amazing with any of the chocolate cookie dough flavors (page 2) as well as the Pumpkin Cookie Dough (page 24).*

Pumpkin Cookie Dough Turnovers

I once showed up to a gathering with a basketful of these pumpkin cookie dough—stuffed turnovers instead of the same-old same-old pumpkin pie I was expected to bring. I was still invited back the next year, as long as I brought the turnovers.

MAKES 8 TURNOVERS

1 (8 x 16) sheet puff pastry, thawed
½ cup Pumpkin Cookie Dough (page 24)
½ cup heavy whipping cream, whipped
½ cup confectioners' sugar
1 tablespoon milk

Preheat the oven to 400°F.

Place the puff pastry sheet on a lightly floured work surface, and cut into 4-inch squares.

Fold the cookie dough into the whipped cream.

Place 2 heaping tablespoons of the cookie dough mixture just a little below the center of the puff pastry. Then fold the top corner of the dough down to meet the opposite corner and press gently to seal. Use a fork to pinch the edges together. Repeat with the remaining dough and filling. Cut 2 vents on the top of each turnover.

Place the turnovers on a parchment-lined baking sheet.

Bake the turnovers for 15 to 20 minutes, or until they are golden brown. Allow them to cool slightly.

While the turnovers are cooling, mix the confectioners' sugar with the milk and stir until smooth, adding a tiny bit more milk, if needed. Drizzle over the turnovers and serve immediately.

TIP! *These turnovers are delicious stuffed with any of the cookie dough flavors.*

Oatmeal Raisin Cookie Dough Tarte Tatin

You'll want a 5-inch ovenproof skillet for this recipe. Well, you'll probably want a 10-inch skillet, because you'll scarf down the 5-inch skillet portion of this caramel-y crumble in about two seconds flat.

MAKES 3 TO 4 SERVINGS

2 tablespoons unsalted butter, at room temperature
2 tablespoons packed light or dark brown sugar
Pinch of salt
2 to 3 medium-size cooking apples, peeled and sliced lengthwise
2 cups Oatmeal Raisin Cookie Dough (page 22)
Vanilla ice cream, for serving (optional)

Preheat the oven to 400°F.

Spread the butter on the bottom of a small (5-inch or so) ovenproof skillet, and cover with the sugar and salt. Add the apples, packing in as many as you can. Place the skillet over medium-high heat, and cook for about 10 minutes, or until the apple juices turn a deep amber. Stir every now and then to make sure the apples get coated with the caramelizing sugar. When the apples are quite soft, remove the skillet from the heat.

While the apples are cooking, roll out the cookie dough to the same size as your skillet. It should be a little less than ½ inch thick. (Too thin, and you'll just end up with cooked cookie dough.)

Place the cookie dough on top of the skillet, tucking it in around the edges. Then place the skillet in the oven for 5 minutes. All you are doing is just slightly warming the cookie dough and giving it a tiny bit of a crust.

Remove the skillet from the oven (be careful—it's hot!), and set on a wire rack. Place a plate on top of the skillet, and with oven-mitted hands, quickly and assertively flip over the skillet. The tarte tatin should come out in all its glistening caramelized glory, with the cookie dough tucked neatly underneath. You may need to give the skillet a bit of a tap on the bottom if it resists.

Serve while warm, with a scoop of vanilla ice cream, if you wish.

TIP! *If oatmeal raisin isn't your thing, cookie dough tarte tatin is also excellent with the Sugar Cookie Dough (page 11), Snickerdoodle Cookie Dough (page 12), or Butterscotch Cookie Dough (page 13).*

Snickerdoodle Cookie Dough Crisp

A gooey layer of cookie dough makes this not quite a crisp, not quite a cobbler, and not quite a crumble. But who cares what it's called when it's this delicious. Stone fruits or something of the apple variety would also be a nice addition.

2 cups fresh or frozen berries
3 tablespoons packed light or dark brown
    sugar, divided
½ cup rolled oats
2 tablespoons unsalted butter, melted
Pinch of salt
1 cup Snickerdoodle Cookie Dough
    (page 12)
Vanilla ice cream, for serving (optional)

Preheat the oven to 400°F.

Place the fruit in the bottom of an 8-inch square baking dish. Sprinkle with 2 tablespoons of the sugar and bake for 10 minutes, or until bubbly.

Mix the oats, butter, remaining 1 tablespoon of sugar, and the salt together.

Drop small spoonfuls of the cookie dough evenly over the fruit, and sprinkle all over with the oat mixture. Bake for 5 minutes, and then broil on high for an additional 2 minutes. All you are doing is just slightly warming the cookie dough to make it oozingly delicious, and browning the crisp topping.

Serve while warm, with a scoop of vanilla ice cream, if you wish.

TIP! *This crisp is delicious with any of the sugar and spice cookie dough flavors (page 10).*

COOKIES & CONFECTIONS

Whether you want your cookie dough dressed to the nines in French Macarons or hanging out in PJs, like the Cookie Dough Fudge, you'll find plenty of little cookie dough bites for sharing (or hoarding).

Sugar Cookie Dough Sandwich Cookies

If there could be such a thing as a cannibalistic cookie, I think this would be it: baked cookie on the outside, raw cookie in the middle. It's the battle of the older, wiser more baked cookie and the young, yet-to-be formed cookie. Who will win? That's easy: you will.

MAKES ABOUT 30 SANDWICH COOKIES

¾ cup all-purpose flour

¼ cup unsweetened Dutch-processed cocoa powder

½ cup packed light or dark brown sugar

Pinch of salt

Pinch of baking soda

6 tablespoons unsalted butter, at room temperature

1 tablespoon milk

1 teaspoon vanilla extract

1 cup Sugar Cookie Dough (page 11)

To make the cookies, combine the flour, cocoa powder, sugar, salt, and baking soda in the bowl of a food processor. Pulse several times to mix thoroughly. Drop in the butter 1 tablespoon at a time and pulse to create a crumbly mixture. Then with the food processor running, drizzle in the milk and vanilla. Pulse until the mixture starts to stick together, about 1 minute.

Preheat the oven to 350°F. Line 2 large baking sheets with parchment paper and set aside. Turn the dough out onto a lightly floured surface. Roll out the dough until it is a little less than ¼ inch thick. Use a 1- to 2-inch round or square cookie cutter to cut out the cookies, and reroll any scraps.

Place the cookies on the baking sheet with at least ½ inch between cookies. Bake until set, 10 to 12 minutes. Allow the cookies to cool completely on a wire rack before filling.

To fill, dollop about a teaspoon of the sugar cookie dough on the flat side of a cookie, and then sandwich with another cookie, giving a little turn to evenly spread the filling.

TIP! *These chocolate wafers are equally good with the Peanut Butter Cookie Dough (page 16) or Chocolate Hazelnut Cookie Dough (page 17) sandwiched between.*

Pistachio-Lemon Cookie Dough—Filled Macarons

For years, I was terrified of French macarons. I assumed that macarons would only work when made on a sunny 70-degree day with eggs laid precisely 83 hours prior and if you hold your breath for 32 minutes. Then I read Stella Parks's (bravetart.com) fantastic essay debunking those crazy macaron myths, slapped myself for believing that baking anything could be that squirrelly, and started piping away. Good thing, or I never would have thought of sandwiching cookie dough between the crisp but chewy shells.

MAKES ABOUT 24 MACARONS

1 cup almond meal

2 cups confectioners' sugar

5 egg whites

⅓ cup granulated sugar

¼ teaspoon salt

1 teaspoon lemon zest

Chopped pistachios, for garnish (optional)

1 cup Pistachio-Lemon Cookie Dough (page 25)

Sift the almond meal and confectioners' sugar together. Set aside. Line 2 sheet pans with parchment paper.

Beat the egg whites, sugar, and salt on medium speed of a stand mixer for 3 minutes. Increase the speed to medium-high, and beat for an additional 3 minutes. Add the lemon zest and increase the speed to high for a final

3 minutes. The meringue should be stiff and dry. If not, beat on high speed for an additional minute.

Fold in the almond mixture, pressing slightly to deflate the meringue against the bowl, 35 to 40 strokes. The batter is ready when it holds a basic shape, but slowly spreads and flattens as it sits.

Transfer the batter to an 18-inch piping bag fitted with a ¼-inch nozzle. Hold the bag straight up and down, and pipe small rounds onto the prepared baking sheets, leaving about an inch between rounds. Garnish the tops with a gentle sprinkle of pistachios. Let the piped batter sit at room temperature for at least 30 minutes.

Preheat the oven to 300°F. Bake each sheet pan for 18 minutes, checking the macarons halfway through baking and rotating. Allow the macarons to cool before removing from the parchment.

Using a spoon, drop a heaping teaspoon of the cookie dough onto the flat side of one macaron shell and then sandwich with another. Macarons can be eaten immediately but are even better the next day.

TIP! *While any cookie dough would make a lovely macaron filling, I like the light nutty sweetness of the pistachio-lemon cookie dough the best.*

Pumpkin Cookie Dough Thumbprint Cookies

Honey, I shrunk the pumpkin pies. . . .

1 cup (2 sticks) unsalted butter, at room temperature
½ cup granulated sugar
2 egg yolks
1 teaspoon vanilla extract
2 cups all-purpose flour
Pinch of salt
1 cup Pumpkin Cookie Dough (page 24)

In a medium bowl, beat the butter and sugar for 3 minutes, until well creamed. Add the egg yolks and vanilla, and beat until creamy. Add the flour and salt and mix, by hand or on low speed with an electric mixer, or until just combined. If it seems too dry, add up to 1 tablespoon of water and pulse until the dough holds together when pinched. Cover and chill the dough for 30 minutes.

Preheat the oven to 350°F.

Scoop out a heaping tablespoon of dough and form it into a ball, and place on a parchment-lined baking sheet. Press down in the center of each dough ball with your thumb to create a small well.

Bake for 12 minutes, or until the dough is just firm. Then remove the baking sheet from the oven, and carefully (don't burn yourself!) fill the well of each still warm cookie with the cookie dough. Let the cookies cool on a wire rack.

TIP! *These little thumbprint cookies taste delicious with any of the cookie doughs in this book.*

Butterscotch Cookie Dough Nanaimo Bars

Ms. Mabel Jenkins holds the honor of creating this chocolate slice bar recipe, which has made the little town of Nanaimo, BC, rather legendary. Her version only went so far as to layer a graham and nut crust with creamy custard and a thick chocolate ganache top. I think she would be rather pleased with the addition of a butterscotch cookie dough layer!

MAKES 16 SMALL BARS

5 tablespoons unsalted butter, divided

2 tablespoons confectioners' sugar

1 large egg

¾ cups graham cracker crumbs

½ cup sweetened shredded coconut

¼ cup pecans, chopped

2 tablespoons unsweetened natural cocoa powder

2 cups Butterscotch Cookie Dough (page 13)

4 ounces unsweetened chocolate, chopped

Preheat the oven to 350°F.

Melt 3 tablespoons of the butter in a heavy-bottomed saucepan over low heat. Let the butter cool for about 3 minutes and then transfer it to the bowl of a food processor. Add the confectioners' sugar and egg. Pulse until well blended. Add the graham cracker crumbs, coconut, pecans, and cocoa powder, and pulse to combine.

Butter a 6-inch square, 2-inch-deep baking pan. Scoop the crumb mixture into the pan, and, using a sheet of waxed paper, gently compress the mixture to even out the top. Bake until slightly darker, about 20 minutes. Let cool completely in the pan.

Spread the butterscotch cookie dough over the baked crust, using an offset spatula to smooth the top.

In a 1- to 2-quart pan over very low heat, stir the remaining 2 tablespoons of butter and the chocolate until melted. Pour over the cookie dough, and then smooth the top. Cover and refrigerate until firm, about 2 hours. Cut into 2-inch bars.

TIP! *The Coconut Macaroon Cookie Dough (page 19), Cashew Caramel Cookie Dough (page 18), or Samoa Cookie Dough (page 7) also make delicious Nanaimo bars.*

Dark Chocolate Gingerbread Cookie Dough Bonbons

Picture yourself on a chaise lounge by the river, gently fanned while you are being fed bonbons by some Greek-physiqued creature. What flavor are the bonbons? If you are lucky, and I'm guessing with that scene you pretty much are, then they are these dark chocolate gingerbread cookie dough beauties.

MAKES 12 TO 15 SMALL BONBONS

½ cup Gingerbread Cookie Dough (page 14)
4 ounces dark chocolate, chopped
1 tablespoon crystallized ginger candy, finely chopped (optional)

Using a small scoop, such as a melon baller, make little orbs of cookie dough, and place them on a waxed paper–lined baking sheet. Chill for 10 to 15 minutes in the freezer, or until firm.

Meanwhile, slowly melt the chocolate in a double boiler (or a metal or glass bowl placed over simmering water), stirring as needed, or until smooth.

Dip each cookie dough ball in the chocolate, and place back on the waxed paper–lined baking sheet. Lightly sprinkle with the crystallized ginger. Allow the bonbons to stand at room temperature to set, about 1 hour. Any bonbons that aren't immediately scarfed down can be stored in the freezer and just lightly thawed when you are ready to eat them later.

TIP! *Bonbons are best when made with any of the cookie doughs that pair well with chocolate, such as the Cashew Caramel Cookie Dough (page 18) or the Samoa Cookie Dough (page 7).*

Samoa Cookie Dough Energy Bars

I like to blame energy bars for my general lack of prolonged physical activity. The mere thought of the "goo" my marathon-running husband consumes by the caseload gives me the shivers. Unfortunately for me, these energy bars do not repulse me. In fact, they pretty much call my name, leaving me no excuse not to lace up my sneakers and go for a run. Darn them.

MAKES 12 (2 X 1-INCH) BARS

½ cup dates, pitted and roughly chopped
½ cup almonds, toasted
¼ cup rolled oats
2 tablespoons flaxseeds
⅛ teaspoon ground cardamom
⅛ teaspoon ground cinnamon
2 teaspoons unsweetened natural
   cocoa powder
⅛ teaspoon vanilla extract
Pinch of salt
¼ cup Samoa Cookie Dough (page 7)

In a food processor, puree the dates, almonds, oats, flaxseeds, cardamom, cinnamon, and cocoa powder into a thick paste. Add the vanilla, salt, and cookie dough and pulse until smooth, 1 to 2 minutes.

Butter a 4 x 6-inch baking pan. Pour the mixture into the pan. Using a sheet of waxed paper, gently compress the mixture to even out the top. Chill for several hours to overnight, until firm, and then slice into 2-inch bars. Store any leftovers in the refrigerator for best results.

Rocky Road Cookie Dough Fudge

I once spent the day photographing a lady make fudge while she showed me all her fudgy secrets, and then she sent me home with more fudge than I could eat in a month. Maybe she hoped all the sugar would make me forget. It didn't. Instead, I borrowed a few of her tricks and put my own spin on the recipe, because the only thing I can imagine that could make a better fudge would be to stir in rich, chunky, chocolaty, nutty cookie dough.

MAKES ABOUT 25 SMALL PIECES OF FUDGE

2 ½ cups granulated sugar
¾ teaspoon salt
4 tablespoons (½ stick) unsalted butter
⅔ cup evaporated milk
12 ounces semisweet chocolate chips
7 ½ ounces marshmallow creme (such as Fluff)
¾ teaspoon vanilla extract
1 cup Rocky Road Cookie Dough (page 8)

Place the sugar, salt, butter, and evaporated milk in a heavy-bottomed pot, and bring to a rolling boil. Continue to boil until the mixture reaches 234°F on an instant-read thermometer, about 5 minutes. Add the chocolate pieces and remove from the heat, and stir to melt. Set aside.

Meanwhile, place the marshmallow creme in the bowl of a stand mixer, and mix briefly to soften. Add the chocolate mixture to the marshmallow and mix well. Add the vanilla and mix again. When smooth, fold in half of the cookie dough. Then, drop in the remaining cookie dough by the spoonful and stir very lightly to coat.

Spread the fudge into a 5-inch square parchment-lined baking pan. Let stand at room temperature until completely cooled. Cut into 1-inch squares to serve.

TIP! *Cookie dough fudge is also delicious with any of the other chocolate (page 2) or nutty cookie doughs (page 15).*

Chocolate and Peanut Butter Cookie Dough Buckeyes

Oh sure, I could go all clichéd on you with this headnote and reference how delicious chocolaty peanut buttery Reese's Peanut Butter Cups are. Well, hmm. I guess I just did.

½ cup Peanut Butter Cookie Dough (page 16)
4 ounces semisweet chocolate chips

Using a small scoop, such as a melon baller, make little orbs of cookie dough, and place them on a waxed paper–lined baking sheet. If the dough is too soft, chill it in the freezer for about 5 minutes first. Chill the formed balls for another 10 to 15 minutes in the freezer, or until firm.

Meanwhile, slowly melt the chocolate in a double boiler (or a metal or glass bowl placed over simmering water), stirring as needed, or until smooth.

Dip each cookie dough ball in the chocolate, leaving a little of the cookie dough exposed on top so they resemble horse chestnuts (a.k.a. buckeyes). Place back on the waxed paper–lined baking sheet, "eye" up. Allow the buckeyes to stand at room temperature to set, about 1 hour. You can refrigerate them to speed up the process.

TIP! *For even more of a twist to the traditional buckeye, try using the Cashew Caramel Cookie Dough (page 18).*

Chocolate Chip Cookie Dough Crispy Rice Treats

Take one bake sale favorite, add in a guilty pleasure, and, well, you won't have them for very long. Better make a double batch.

MAKES 12 BARS

3 tablespoons unsalted butter

10 ounces marshmallows (about 40)

6 cups puffed rice cereal

1 cup Chocolate Chip Cookie Dough (page 3)

. . . .

Melt the butter in a heavy-bottomed saucepan over low heat, adding the marshmallows and stirring until completely melted. Stir in the puffed rice cereal.

Butter a 9 x 5-inch loaf pan. Scoop half of the sticky puffed rice mixture into the pan. Drop spoonfuls of the chocolate chip cookie dough on top. Then, top with the remaining sticky puffed rice. Place a sheet of waxed paper over the top and then gently compress the mixture to even out the top. Let cool and cut into 3-inch bars.

TIP! *Crispy rice treats are also great when made with the Coconut Macaroon Cookie Dough (page 19), Snickerdoodle Cookie Dough (page 12), or Rocky Road Cookie Dough (page 8).*

Cashew Caramel Cookie Dough Candy Bars

Those wimpy store-bought cookies and cream bars never had a chance. This is the cookie dough candy bar you've always dreamed about: a thick bite of doughy cashew and caramel blanketed in chocolate. Warning: Do not give these out at Halloween, or chances are you may have hordes of wily parents knocking adorably costumed children out of the way to snatch up a few of these babies.

MAKES 3 (1 X 3-INCH) BARS

1 cup Cashew Caramel Cookie Dough (page 18)
4 ounces dark chocolate or milk chocolate baking chips

Place the cookie dough between 2 sheets of waxed paper, and gently press or roll out the dough into a ¾-inch-thick square or rectangle. Chill for 15 minutes in the freezer, or until firm. Cut the chilled dough into 1 x 3-inch rectangles (or any shape you desire!). Place each bar on a waxed paper–lined baking sheet and chill the pan in the freezer for 10 minutes.

Meanwhile, slowly melt the chocolate in a double boiler (or a metal or glass bowl placed over simmering water), stirring as needed, or until smooth.

Dip each cookie dough bar in the chocolate, and place back on the waxed paper–lined baking sheet. Allow the bars to stand at room temperature to set, about 1 hour. You can refrigerate them to speed the process. Serve whole, or chop each bar into thirds for bite-size pieces to share.

TIP! *For a Mounds-like candy bar, try using the Coconut Macaroon Cookie Dough (page 19).*

Chocolate Cookie Dough "Cooksie" Pops

Just how many licks does it take to get to the doughy center of these cookie dough cooksie pops? You'll just have to try them to find out!

MAKES 14 TO 16 POPS

1 cup Chocolate Wafer Cookie Dough
    (page 5)
1 cup granulated sugar
⅓ cup light corn syrup
¼ teaspoon cream of tartar
Pinch of salt
½ teaspoon vanilla extract or candy
    flavoring of your choice
Drop of liquid food coloring (optional)

Using a small scoop, such as a melon baller, make little orbs of cookie dough, and place them on a waxed paper–lined baking sheet. Stick a lollipop stick into the top of each one. Chill for 10 to 15 minutes in the freezer, or until firm.

When the cookie dough is firm, make the candy coating. Place the sugar, corn syrup, ½ cup of water, the cream of tartar, and the salt in a saucepan over medium heat, stir until just mixed, and then cook until the sugar has dissolved. Do not stir once the sugar begins to boil. Cook until the syrup reaches

300°F on an instant-read thermometer. It will take about 15 minutes, but keep a close eye on it so it doesn't bubble over or exceed 300°F.

Remove the pan from the heat, and let cool to 275°F. Add the vanilla and food coloring, if using.

Working quickly at this point, dip each cookie dough ball into the syrup to coat it completely, and then hold it above the pot to drain off any excess syrup. Place the pop back on the lined baking sheet, stick up, to set. Repeat the process with the remaining cookie dough balls. Let the pops cool completely before serving.

Sugar Cookie Dough Truffles

It's hardly fair that truffles so easy to whip up can be this freaking good. Throw some flour in your hair or something so everyone will think you had to put in at least an ounce of effort.

½ cup Sugar Cookie Dough (page 11)
1 cup unsweetened natural cocoa
   powder
¼ cup confectioners' sugar

Using a small scoop, such as a melon baller, make little orbs of cookie dough, and place them on a waxed paper–lined baking sheet. Chill for 10 to 15 minutes in the freezer, or until firm.

Meanwhile, sift the cocoa powder and sugar in a bowl.

Roll each cookie dough ball in the cocoa mixture to cover completely. Serve immediately.

TIP! *Cookie dough truffles are outstanding with just about any cookie dough that would taste good with chocolate. For me, that would be all of them!*

Yogurt-Covered Cranberry Apple Cookie Dough Pops

The thing about yogurt is that you can put it on anything and suddenly you have healthy food. And with the cranberries and apples, these pops are quite in danger of losing their junk food status.

MAKES 8 TO 10 POPS

½ cup Cranberry Apple Cookie Dough (page 23)
1¾ cups confectioners' sugar
1 teaspoon light corn syrup
Pinch of salt
1 teaspoon vanilla extract
¼ cup Greek-style whole-milk plain yogurt
1 tablespoon granulated sugar
¼ teaspoon agar powder

Using a small scoop, such as a melon baller, make little orbs of cookie dough, and place them on a waxed paper–lined baking sheet. Chill for 10 to 15 minutes in the freezer, or until firm.

Mix the confectioners' sugar, corn syrup, salt, vanilla, and yogurt in the bowl of a stand mixer fitted with a paddle attachment until smooth.

Mix the granulated sugar, agar, and 1 teaspoon of water in a small ramekin and microwave for about 30 seconds on full power, or until a thin syrup is formed.

With your mixer on low, stream the agar syrup into the confectioners' sugar mixture and mix until smooth, about 2 minutes, scraping down the sides of the bowl as needed.

To make the pops, dip a lollipop stick into the yogurt coating, and then carefully insert it about halfway into a dough ball. Holding onto the stick, dip each cookie dough ball in the yogurt coating, and then insert the stick into a Styrofoam block to keep it upright. Allow the pops to stand at room temperature to set, about 1 hour. You can refrigerate them to speed up the process.

TIP! *Any of the cookie dough flavors would be delicious as yogurt-covered cookie dough pops.*

ICE CREAM & FROZEN TREATS

Whether you make your own custard base (or simply shortcut with store-bought ice cream), ice cream with cookie dough smashed in is oh so fine. So, pull out the cones, bowls, spoons, and straws, and dive on in.

Cookie Dough and Cream Ice Cream

You'll have heaps of chocolate and white stuffing goodness in this ice cream without all the hassle of the twisting and splitting you get with Oreos. There's still plenty of licking though.

MAKES A LITTLE LESS THAN 1 QUART

2 cups heavy whipping cream, divided

⅓ cup granulated sugar

1 tablespoon light corn syrup or golden syrup

½ teaspoon salt, plus a pinch

1 cup whole milk

1½ teaspoons vanilla extract, divided

4 tablespoons (½ stick) unsalted butter, at room temperature

2 tablespoons unsalted butter, melted

½ cup confectioners' sugar

½ cup Chocolate Wafer Cookie Dough (page 5)

Place 1 cup of the cream in a pot with the granulated sugar, corn syrup, and ½ teaspoon of the salt and cook over medium-low heat, or until the sugar dissolves and the mixture thickens just slightly. Stir in the remaining cup of cream, the milk, and 1 teaspoon of the vanilla, and place the mixture in the refrigerator to chill, covered, for at least 1 hour. Then churn according to your ice-cream maker's directions until the ice cream is thick.

While the ice cream is churning, make the "white stuffing" by creaming the room-temperature butter, melted butter, remaining ½ teaspoon of vanilla, and a pinch of salt until smooth. Then, gradually add the confectioners' sugar until fully incorporated.

Transfer the ice cream to a freezer-safe container, layering with a spoonful of the cookie dough and spoonfuls of the white stuffing as you go. Freeze for at least 2 hours, or until firm, before scooping and serving.

TIP! *Make the "thin mint" version of the chocolate wafer cookie dough (page 5) for the best ever chocolate mint cookie ice cream!*

Butterscotch Cookie Dough Ice-Cream Sandwiches

These ice-cream sandwiches may not transport you back to your childhood with those cardboardlike chocolate wafers filled with vanilla ice cream, but crisp graham crackers smeared with butterscotch cookie dough ice cream tastes way better than nostalgia.

MAKES 4 (4 X 6-INCH) SANDWICHES

2 cups heavy whipping cream, divided
⅓ cup granulated sugar
1 tablespoon light corn syrup or golden syrup
½ teaspoon salt
1 cup milk
½ cup Butterscotch Cookie Dough (page 13)
8 4 x 6-inch graham crackers or your favorite cookies

Place 1 cup of the cream in a pot with the sugar, corn syrup, and salt and cook over medium-low heat, or until the sugar dissolves and the mixture thickens just slightly. Stir in the remaining cup of cream and the milk, and place the mixture in the refrigerator to chill, covered, for at least 1 hour. Then churn according to your ice-cream maker's directions until the ice cream has just started to thicken. Then drop in the cookie dough by the tablespoon. Continue to churn until thick.

Line a small jelly-roll pan (about 13 x 9 inches, or one that will fit into your freezer) with parchment paper hanging over opposite sides of the pan about 2 inches, forming handles. You can also use a couple of cake or tart pans, if the jelly-roll pan is too big.

Spread the ice cream about a little more than ½ inch thick over the parchment.

Cover with more parchment, and freeze overnight. When frozen solid, flip over the pan onto a cutting board (marble is perfect if you have one!), and cut out the ice cream with a cookie cutter or knife to fit your graham crackers or cookies. Sandwich the ice cream between 2 cookies and return to the freezer for about 15 minutes (or place in a resealable plastic bag and store for up to 1 week).

TIP! *Any of the spiced cookie dough flavors (page 10) will work well in these ice-cream sandwiches.*

Samoa Cookie Dough Coconut Ice Cream

Coconut milk makes this deconstructed cookie ice cream exceptionally silky in between the big ol' chunks of chocolate coconut cookie dough and swirls of caramel.

2 cups heavy whipping cream, divided
⅓ cup granulated sugar
1 tablespoon light corn syrup or golden syrup
½ teaspoon salt
1 cup coconut milk
½ cup Samoa Cookie Dough (page 7)

Place 1 cup of the cream in a pot with the sugar, corn syrup, and salt and cook over medium-low heat, or until the sugar dissolves and the mixture thickens just slightly. Turn off the heat, stir in the remaining cup of cream and the coconut milk, and transfer the mixture to a covered container. Place the ice-cream base in the refrigerator to chill, covered, for at least 1 hour. Then churn according to your ice-cream maker's directions until the ice cream is thick.

Transfer the ice cream to a freezer-safe container, layering with spoonfuls of the cookie dough as you go. Freeze for at least 2 hours, or until firm, before scooping and serving.

TIP! *Any of the cookie dough flavors will work well in this recipe.*

Pistachio-Lemon Cookie Dough Sorbet

Creamy isn't normally how you'd describe a sorbet, but this one is unapologetically so. You might be tempted to call it ice cream, but with no milk or cream (just a bit of luscious mascarpone), it really isn't that, either. All you should really care about, though, is that it's on a spoon and in your mouth.

MAKES ABOUT 1 PINT

1 cup granulated sugar
Zest and juice of 1 lemon
½ cup mascarpone, at room temperature
½ cup Pistachio-Lemon Cookie Dough
    (page 25)

. . . .

In a medium saucepan, combine the sugar, 1 cup of water, and the lemon zest and juice over medium heat. Bring to a boil, reduce the heat, and simmer for 2 minutes, stirring occasionally, or until the sugar has dissolved. Remove the pan from the heat and allow the syrup to cool, about 20 minutes.

Add the mascarpone and cookie dough to the syrup, and blend with an immersion blender or food processor until mostly smooth, 1 to 2 minutes. Transfer the mixture to a small loaf pan, about 4 x 6 inches. Cover and freeze for at least 4 hours, or until firm, before scooping and serving.

TIP! *You can also use cream cheese or Neufchâtel in place of the mascarpone, for delicious results.*

Snickerdoodle Cookie Dough Ice Pops

Warm cookies and milk aren't exactly what you crave when the thermometer starts to creep over 80°F (yes, those of us in the Pacific Northwest think that's hot!), but these snickerdoodles-on-a-stick sure hit the spot. Plus, they are a snap to make and great to have on hand for when the craving hits!

MAKES 8 (4-OUNCE) ICE POPS

2 cups heavy whipping cream, divided
⅓ cup granulated sugar
1 tablespoon light corn syrup or golden syrup
½ teaspoon salt
1 cup whole milk
1 cup Snickerdoodle Cookie Dough (page 12)

Place 1 cup of the cream in a pot with the sugar, corn syrup, and salt and cook over medium-low heat, or until the sugar dissolves and the mixture thickens just slightly. Stir in the remaining cup of cream and the milk, and place the mixture in the refrigerator to chill, covered, for at least 1 hour.

Place the chilled cream mixture and the cookie dough into the bowl of a stand mixer and stir together until it is just partly mixed, so nothing is too runny but there are still some cookie dough clumps.

Spoon the mixture into ice pop molds and freeze for at least 4 hours, or until firm, before serving. Kept frozen and covered, they keep up to 2 weeks.

TIP! *Any of the cookie dough flavors will work well in this recipe.*

Pumpkin Cookie Dough Ice Cream

No need to go all pumpkin-crazy serving this rich pumpkin cookie dough ice cream along with some other pumpkiny cake or pie. It's plenty of pumpkin all on its own.

MAKES A LITTLE LESS THAN A QUART

2 cups heavy whipping cream, divided
⅓ cup granulated sugar
1 tablespoon light corn syrup or golden syrup
½ teaspoon salt
1 cup whole milk
1 teaspoon vanilla extract
1 cup Pumpkin Cookie Dough (page 24)

Place 1 cup of the cream in a pot with the sugar, corn syrup, and salt and cook over medium-low heat, or until the sugar dissolves and the mixture thickens just slightly. Stir in the remaining cup of cream and the milk and vanilla, and place the mixture in the refrigerator to chill, covered, for at least 1 hour. Once cool, blend the ice-cream base with the pumpkin cookie dough in a blender or food processor until fully incorporated. Chill for 1 hour, and then churn according to your ice-cream maker's directions until the ice cream is thick.

Transfer the ice cream to a freezer-safe container. Freeze for at least 2 hours, or until firm, before scooping and serving.

Chocolate Cherry Cookie Dough Parfait

Is there anything more fun than a layered dessert? Sure, you could win the lottery and travel around the world for a year. That would be more fun. Or, you could be in a bathtub full of puppies. But that aside, this chocolate cherry cookie dough parfait is pretty darn high on the fun factor—and far easier to attain.

MAKES 1 PARFAIT

¼ cup chocolate wafer cookies, crushed
½ cup vanilla ice cream or frozen yogurt
½ cup fresh or frozen cherries, chopped
2 tablespoons Chocolate Cherry Cookie Dough (page 9)
Whipped cream, for garnish
1 fresh or maraschino cherry, for garnish

Place a heaping spoonful of the chocolate wafer cookies in the bottom of a tall parfait glass. Drop in a small scoop of ice cream. Add a spoonful of the chopped cherries. Add the cookie dough, and gently push down and smooth with the back of a spoon. Add the remaining ice cream, followed by the remaining crushed wafer cookies and the cherries. Top with whipped cream and a cherry.

TIP! *Any of the chocolate cookie dough recipes (page 2) would work beautifully in this parfait.*

Coconut Macaroon Cookie Dough Sundae

When's the last time you made a sundae at home? I have the fondest memories of making ginormous banana splits slathered in chocolate fudge sauce with my friends in elementary school (back when we walked uphill both ways to school), but somehow I fell out of the habit of such indulgences, so this sundae was a particular treat.

MAKES 1 SUNDAE

1 scoop vanilla ice cream or frozen yogurt
1 scoop chocolate ice cream or frozen yogurt
2 tablespoons Coconut Macaroon Cookie Dough (page 19)
2 tablespoons chocolate fudge sauce, warmed
Whipped cream, for garnish
1 fresh or maraschino cherry, for garnish

Place one small scoop of each ice cream in a chilled sundae bowl. Place the cookie dough between the 2 scoops. Drizzle with the chocolate fudge sauce. Top with whipped cream and a cherry.

Oatmeal Raisin Cookie Dough Thick Shake

These thick shakes (milk shakes without the milk) can be compared to your favorite DQ Blizzard, but these shakes are reasonably sized so you aren't stuck with melty-melt for your last sips. They are also pure oatmeal deliciousness. Spoons may be required.

MAKES 2 SMALL THICK SHAKES

1 cup vanilla ice cream (or your favorite flavor)
¼ cup Oatmeal Raisin Cookie Dough (page 22)

Place the ice cream and cookie dough in a blender and pulse once or twice to blend (or more if you prefer a more evenly distributed shake). Serve immediately.

TIP! *Any of the cookie dough flavors makes for a delicious blizzard.*

Mocha Brownie Cookie Dough Shake

Mix and match cookie doughs and ice cream flavors to your taste to discover your favorite cookie dough flavor shake. But, do try this ridiculously rich combination of coffee ice cream and brownie cookie dough when you are feeling particularly extravagant.

MAKES 1 SHAKE

1 cup coffee ice cream (or your favorite flavor)
¼ cup milk
½ cup Brownie Cookie Dough (page 6)

Place the ice cream, milk, and cookie dough in a blender and pulse once or twice to blend (or more if you prefer a more evenly distributed shake). Serve immediately.

Cashew Caramel Cookie Dough Chocolate Ice Cream

My husband doesn't like chocolate ice cream, but he loves caramel and cashews, so I have to hide this delicious recipe from him all the same.

MAKES A LITTLE LESS THAN A QUART

2 cups heavy whipping cream, divided

⅓ cup granulated sugar

1 tablespoon light corn syrup or golden syrup

⅓ cup unsweetened natural cocoa powder

½ teaspoon salt

1 cup whole milk

1 teaspoon vanilla extract

½ cup Cashew Caramel Cookie Dough (page 18)

Place 1 cup of the cream in a pot with the sugar, corn syrup, cocoa powder, and salt and cook over medium-low heat, or until the sugar dissolves and the mixture thickens just slightly. Stir in the remaining cup of cream and the milk and vanilla, and place the mixture in the refrigerator to chill, covered, for at least 1 hour. Then churn according to your ice-cream maker's directions until the ice cream is thick.

Transfer the ice cream to a freezer-safe container, layering with spoonfuls of the cookie dough as you go. Freeze for at least 2 hours, or until firm, before scooping and serving.

TIP! *Any of the chocolate (page 2) or nutty cookie dough flavors (page 15) will work well in this recipe.*

REALLY WILD STUFF

This chapter is a playground of cookie dough recipes, where imagination turns everyday treats into feats of whimsy. Monkey bread (page 129), fluffernutters (page 117), and profiteroles (page 149) are eaten with abandon, while such goodies as Peanut Butter Cookie Dough—Stuffed Pretzels (page 141) are secretly squirreled away for the leaner times.

Peanut Butter Cookie Dough Fluffernutter

This fluffernutter is like a fairy dream of sandwiches from a world where rivers run with chocolate, clouds are poufs of cotton candy, and the fruit and vegetable serving on your dinner plate is Skittles. This fluffernutter is that good.

MAKES 1 SANDWICH

2 slices white bread

3 tablespoons Peanut Butter Cookie Dough (page 16)

3 tablespoons marshmallow creme (such as Fluff)

1 banana, sliced

Spread the cookie dough on one slice of bread and the marshmallow creme on the other. Place the banana slices on top of the cookie dough, and sandwich the 2 pieces of bread together. Eat!

TIP! *Want it even more decadent? Use the chocolate hazelnut cookie dough (page 17).*

Samoa Cookie Dough Egg Rolls

I love when you take something you expect to be savory and twist it up into something sweet. These egg rolls fit that bill perfectly. Tucked away inside the crisp shell is a hidden caramel, coconut, and chocolate surprise.

MAKES 8 SMALL EGG ROLLS

8 (8-inch square) egg roll wrappers
½ cup Samoa Cookie Dough (page 7)
Oil, for frying

Fill a small ramekin with water and set it near you.

On a clean, dry surface, lay out an egg roll wrapper with one corner pointing toward you. Shape a heaping tablespoon of cookie dough into a small log, about 2 inches long and ½-inch-thick, and place about an inch from the point of the corner. Lift the corner and roll the wrapper around the cookie dough, or until the wrapper is almost half rolled. Fold the side corners in toward the center and continue to roll, tucking in the sides as you roll. Dip your fingers in the water, and lightly moisten the top corner.

Finish rolling and press to seal, using a bit more water if needed.

Place the eggroll on a parchment-lined baking sheet, and cover with a kitchen towel. Repeat with the remaining wrappers. The filled rolls can be refrigerated for up to 4 hours, until ready to fry or freeze.

To fry the egg rolls, fill a heavy-bottomed pot with 2 inches of oil, and cook over medium heat at 350°F. Gently slide in or lower in the egg rolls, frying 4 to 6 at a time, turning occasionally until golden brown, about 1 ½ minutes. Place on a wire rack to drain and let cool.

TIP! *If you have leftover egg roll wrappers, they are great fried as crackers (maybe to serve alongside the Chocolate Chip Cookie Dough Dip, page 145), or you can freeze the remaining wrappers in a resealable plastic bag, and then thaw before using.*

Deep-Fried Chocolate Chip Cookie Dough

Want to freak out your food snob friends? Serve them deep-fried cookie dough for dessert and watch them squirm. And then call you a genius.

MAKES ABOUT 16 FRITTERS

1 cup Chocolate Chip Cookie Dough
   (page 3)
½ cup all-purpose flour
2 tablespoons granulated sugar
½ teaspoon baking powder
Pinch of salt
½ cup club soda
1 large egg white
½ teaspoon vanilla extract
Oil, for frying
Confectioners' sugar, for dusting (optional)

Using a small scoop, such as a melon baller, make little orbs of cookie dough, and place them on a waxed paper–lined baking sheet. Chill for at least 15 minutes in the freezer, or until firm.

In large bowl, whisk together the flour, sugar, baking powder, and salt. In a medium bowl, whisk together the club soda, egg white, and vanilla. Whisk the wet ingredients into the dry. Remove the frozen cookie dough balls from the freezer.

In a heavy-bottomed pot over medium-high heat, heat 4 inches of oil until an instant-read thermometer registers 350°F. Dip 4 of the cookie dough balls in the batter and turn to coat, shaking off any excess batter. Carefully transfer the coated balls to the hot oil, and fry until golden brown, 1 to 2 minutes. Transfer to paper towels to drain, and repeat with the remaining dough balls.

Serve the fritters warm, with a little dusting of confectioners' sugar, if desired.

Cashew Caramel Cookie Dough Flautas

Turn your Cinco de Mayo celebration into a Cookie Dough Mayo party with these quick-to-make (and eat) cookie dough flautas. Cashew caramel cookie dough is particularly amazing tucked away in the fried tortilla, but for a party, try spreading the tortillas with different doughs for a fun variety.

MAKES 24 FLAUTA BITES, OR 8 WHOLE FLAUTAS

8 (8-inch) flour tortillas
1 cup Cashew Caramel Cookie Dough, softened (page 18)
Oil, for frying
Confectioners' sugar, for dusting

On a clean, dry surface, lay out one flour tortilla. Prick it all over with a fork. (This will help keep it from developing air pockets as it fries.) Place 2 tablespoons of cookie dough about ¾ inch from the edge, and gently spread toward the edges, leaving a ¾-inch gap. Lift the bottom of the tortilla and roll it around the cookie dough, or until the tortilla is almost half rolled. Fold the side corners in to meet at the center, continue to roll, tucking in the edges as you roll. When the tortilla is completely rolled, secure the ends with toothpicks.

Place the tortilla on a parchment-lined baking sheet, and cover with a kitchen towel. Repeat with the remaining tortillas. The filled rolls can be refrigerated up to 4 hours until ready to fry.

To fry the flautas, fill a heavy-bottomed pot with 2 inches of oil, and cook over medium heat at 350°F. Gently slide the rolls into the oil, frying 2 to 3 at a time, turning occasionally until golden brown, about 1 ½ minutes. Place on a wire rack to drain and let cool. Slice each flauta into thirds to create flauta bites, if desired. Serve with a dusting of confectioners' sugar.

Cranberry Apple Cookie Dough Aebleskivers

Part pancake, part doughnut hole, these magical Danish treats typically hide little bits of jam or sautéed apples, so a little gem of cranberry apple cookie dough tucked inside seems like the perfect match.

MAKES 14 AEBLESKIVERS

1 ¼ cups all-purpose flour

3 tablespoons granulated sugar

1 tablespoon baking powder

¼ teaspoon salt

¼ teaspoon ground cardamom

1 large egg

1 cup milk

4 to 5 tablespoons unsalted butter, melted, divided

About ½ cup Cranberry Apple Cookie Dough (page 23)

In a medium bowl, mix the flour, sugar, baking powder, salt, and cardamom. In a small bowl or measuring cup, whisk the egg with the milk and 2 tablespoons of the melted butter. Stir the wet ingredients into the flour, and stir just to incorporate. It's easiest to then transfer the mixture to a pitcher, so you don't have to spoon into each cup. Set aside.

Scoop 14 ½ teaspoon–size balls of the cookie dough and place them on waxed paper.

Warm a cast-iron aebleskiver pan over medium-high heat for about 3 minutes. Generously brush each cup with some of the remaining butter, and reduce the heat to medium. Pour the batter into each cup until halfway full. Place a ball of dough in the center and then top with a bit more batter, filling to just below the rim. Cook until the edges turn golden and pull slightly away from the edge of the pan. Insert a skewer into the batter, and gently pull up on the side to rotate the pancake about a quarter-turn. If the pancake seems stuck, run the skewer around the edges to loosen it.

Cook for another minute, and pull with the skewer to rotate another quarter-turn. Repeat this process until the pancake is cooked on the outside, forming a neat little ball. Continue to cook for another 1 to 2 minutes to cook through. Repeat with the remaining batter. Serve warm. Traditionally you'd give them a shake of confectioners' sugar or a bit of syrup, but the cookie dough will provide enough sweetness that you may not find it necessary.

TIP! *Any of the cookie dough recipes makes an amazing aebleskiver filling.*

Chocolate Espresso Cookie Dough Monkey Bread

The ooey-gooey espresso caramel that coats each biscuit ball would likely be enough to make you silly for this pull-apart dessert. But the hidden chocolate espresso cookie dough surprise in the middle of each ball? Now that's just ridiculous.

MAKES 8 TO 10 SERVINGS

½ cup (1 stick) unsalted butter, plus more for buttering pan

2 cups Chocolate Espresso Cookie Dough (page 4)

⅓ cup granulated sugar

2 (16-ounce) cans refrigerated biscuits

1 cup packed light or dark brown sugar

2 tablespoons espresso, room temperature

Preheat the oven to 350°F. Butter an 8 x 10-inch Bundt pan or a baking pan with fluted sides and set aside.

Roll teaspoon-size orbs of cookie dough (32 of them), and place them on a waxed paper–lined baking sheet. Chill for 10 to 15 minutes in the freezer, until firm.

Place the granulated sugar in a shallow bowl. Cut each uncooked biscuit in half, and then wrap each half around a ball of the cookie dough. Roll in the sugar, and place in the bottom of the prepared pan. Make another, slightly larger layer of dough balls on top with the remaining biscuit and cookie dough pieces, pressing down lightly on each dough ball as you wedge it into place.

In a small saucepan, melt the ½ cup of butter with the brown sugar and espresso over medium-low heat until completely melted. Then pour evenly on top of the biscuit balls.

Bake for 35 minutes. Let the bread cool in the pan for 10 minutes, and then turn out onto a cake plate to serve.

TIP! *Not a fan of canned biscuits? You can use your favorite biscuit dough; just make sure it makes about 16 large biscuits.*

Oatmeal Cookie Dough Porridge

A dollop of oatmeal cookie dough and a splash of cold milk make this breakfast porridge remarkably like sitting down to fresh-from-the-oven cookies and milk.

MAKES 2 BOWLS

1 cup milk
1 teaspoon salt
1 cup steel-cut oats
1 ½ tablespoons packed light or dark brown sugar
2 heaping tablespoons Oatmeal Raisin Cookie Dough (page 22)
Cold milk, for serving (optional)

Mix 1 cup of water, the milk, and the salt in a heavy-bottomed pot over medium-high heat and bring just to a boil. Stream in the oats, stirring as you pour. Lower the heat slightly, to keep at a simmer, and cook, stirring on occasion, for about 25 minutes, or until the oats have softened to a tender bite. Stir in the brown sugar.

Divide between 2 bowls, and top each with a tablespoon of cookie dough. If desired, pour a bit of cold milk around the edges.

TIP! *Any of the spice- (page 10) or fruit-based cookie doughs (page 21) work great as a porridge topper.*

Snickerdoodle Cookie Dough Cinnamon Rolls

These heavenly little cinnamon rolls are almost as easy as popping open a can, but with the magic of cookie dough rolled in. The longer cooking time firms the cookie dough slightly, giving each roll a soft cookie bite.

MAKES 8 CINNAMON ROLLS

1 ¼ cups all-purpose flour

2 teaspoons baking powder

½ teaspoon baking soda

¼ teaspoon salt

½ cup ricotta cheese

¼ cup milk

4 tablespoons granulated sugar, divided

2 tablespoons unsalted butter, at room temperature, plus 2 tablespoons, melted

1 teaspoon vanilla extract

1 cup Snickerdoodle Cookie Dough (page 12)

⅛ teaspoon ground cinnamon

Preheat the oven to 350°F. Spray an 8- or 9-inch baking dish with baking spray and set aside.

Sift the flour, baking powder, baking soda, and salt in a small bowl and set aside.

In the bowl of a stand mixer, blend the ricotta, milk, 2 tablespoons of the sugar, the room-temperature butter, and the vanilla. Add the flour mixture, and stir just until blended.

Turn out the dough onto a lightly floured surface, and knead 4 or 5 times to form a smooth dough. Then roll out to an 8 x 10-inch rectangle about ¼-inch-thick, and brush with the 2 tablespoons of melted butter, saving just a little to brush the tops.

Spread the cookie dough evenly over the surface of the rolled dough. Roll the dough into a 10-inch-long log, and pinch the seam to seal. Trim the ends and slice into 8 pieces, and place them cut-side up into the prepared baking dish, dough sides just touching. There will be some space between the rolls and the edge of the pan.

In a small bowl, mix together the remaining 2 tablespoons of sugar with the cinnamon.

Brush the tops and sides of each roll with a bit more butter and sprinkle with the cinnamon-sugar mixture. Bake for 25 to 35 minutes, or until the edges are golden. Let cool only slightly before serving.

Pumpkin Cookie Dough Waffles

Now, I know I told you that you didn't need to go all pumpkin-crazy with that pumpkin ice cream on page 105, but now I'm taking it back. While these pumpkin waffles are perfectly delicious with a drizzle of syrup and a side of bacon, they are insanely good if you pair them with a scoop of that pumpkin cookie dough ice cream.

MAKES 4 TO 6 WAFFLES

1 cup Pumpkin Cookie Dough (page 24)
1 ½ teaspoons baking powder
2 teaspoons cornstarch
1 large egg
½ cup buttermilk
2 tablespoons unsalted butter, melted,
    plus more for waffle iron

Place the cookie dough, baking powder, cornstarch, and egg in the bowl of a stand mixer. Beat on medium speed for about 2 minutes, or until smooth. Stream in the buttermilk and melted butter and beat until the mixture is smooth.

Brush the waffle iron with butter and heat.

Pour about ⅓ cup (or the amount recommended by the manufacturer's directions) of batter onto each waffle iron. Close the lid of the waffle maker and cook for about 3 minutes or until waffles are golden brown. Repeat with the remaining batter, and serve immediately.

TIP! *These waffles taste great with just about any of the cookie dough flavors.*

Baked Sugar Cookie Dough—Stuffed Apples

With apple for crust and cookie dough for filling, these inside-out treats are even easier than pie!

6 medium-size Granny Smith apples
¼ cup granulated sugar
½ teaspoon ground cinnamon
6 tablespoons Sugar Cookie Dough
   (page 11)
1 pint vanilla ice cream (optional)

Preheat the oven to 350°F.

With a paring knife, cut the "lid" off each apple, about ½ inch thick. Then, using an apple corer or melon baller, scoop out the seedy core and just a bit of the surrounding flesh.

Mix the sugar and cinnamon together.

Place the apples upright on a parchment-lined baking sheet and bake for about 15 minutes. Remove the apples from the oven, and stuff each with a heaping tablespoon of cookie dough. Sprinkle the tops of each with the cinnamon-sugar mixture, and top with the apple "lid." Bake for another 15 minutes, until the tops of the apples brown slightly. Then broil for 2 to 3 minutes to caramelize.

Remove from the oven, and let cool slightly before serving. Top each with a scoop of ice cream, if desired.

TIP! *These apples taste great when stuffed with any of the sugar and spice (page 10) or fruit-based (page 21) cookie dough flavors.*

Peanut Butter Cookie Dough—Stuffed Pretzels

A bowl full of peanut butter cookie dough—stuffed pretzels set in the middle of a table is a rare thing. Put one down, and suddenly, almost faster than you can say, "Peanut butter cookie dough—stuffed pretzels, anyone?" all you'll have is an empty bowl.

MAKES ABOUT 50 STUFFED PRETZEL BITES

1 package (0.25-ounce) active dry yeast
1 teaspoon granulated sugar
3½ cups bread flour, divided
½ teaspoon salt
¼ cup baking soda
1 cup Peanut Butter Cookie Dough (page 16)
2 egg whites
¼ cup coarse sea salt (or seasoning of your choice)

In the bowl of a stand mixer, combine 1 cup of warm water, the yeast, and the sugar. Mix well and let stand for 5 minutes. Add half of the bread flour and the salt, and stir to create a slack dough. Using a dough hook attachment, with the mixer on low speed, add the remaining bread flour a little at a time until the dough comes together into a ball. Increase the mixer speed to high and beat for 3 minutes. Punch down the dough, and continue to knead with the dough hook, at a medium-low speed, for another 2 minutes, or until the dough is smooth and not sticky.

Cover the dough and let it rise for 1 hour in a warm spot (70°–80°F). Preheat the oven to 250°F.

While the dough is rising, spread the baking soda on an aluminum foil–lined baking sheet and bake for 1 hour at 250°F. This will make the baking soda a bit stronger and give more of a pretzel flavor to your snacks. This makes a bit more baked soda than you need, but it keeps well in a sealed jar.

Increase the oven temperature to 350°F.

Divide the dough into 4 pieces. Working with one piece at a time (leaving the rest covered), on a generously floured surface, roll out to a very thin sheet, a little less than ¼ inch. Cut the dough

into about 50 (1½-inch) squares. Place ¼ teaspoon of the peanut butter cookie dough in the center of the pretzel dough, and roll around the peanut butter cookie dough, pinching the edges together. Place them seam-side down on a parchment-lined baking sheet.

Whisk together the egg whites, 2 tablespoons of water, and 1 tablespoon of the baked baking soda. Brush each pretzel generously with the mixture, and sprinkle with the coarse sea salt (or seasoning of your choice).

Bake for about 20 minutes, rotating the baking sheet halfway through baking, or until the pretzels are a deep golden brown. Let cool on a wire rack.

TIP! *These pretzels are also amazing with chocolate hazelnut cookie dough (page 17).*

Gingerbread Cookie Dough "Crème" Brûlée

There may be nothing "crème" about this brûlée, but the slightly soft, warm gingerbread dough is so stunningly good, you really won't care. Plus, it's just so much fun to crack through the sugar crust to scoop up every last bite.

MAKES 4 BRÛLÉES

1 cup Gingerbread Cookie Dough (page 14)
½ cup granulated sugar

. . . .

Divide the cookie dough evenly among 4 shallow ramekins, and spread smoothly with an offset spatula. Sprinkle 2 tablespoons of sugar evenly over each ramekin, and place the ramekins on a baking sheet.

Heat the broiler with the rack set so that the ramekins will be about 2 inches from the heat. Broil for 1 to 2 minutes, or until the sugar has caramelized. Let the brûlées set for about 5 minutes to allow the topping to crisp up.

TIP! *This brûlée is delicious with almost any of the cookie doughs!*

Chocolate Chip Cookie Dough Dip or Spread

It may not sound like there is much to this spread, but the sum is definitely more than its parts. Serve with graham crackers or vanilla wafers, spread on pancakes and top with a sliced banana, or even try a celery stick full to add a little decadence to an otherwise plain snack.

MAKES ABOUT ½ CUP SPREAD

¼ cup Chocolate Chip Cookie Dough
   (page 3)
1 tablespoon cream cheese, at room
   temperature
1 tablespoon plain yogurt

Place the cookie dough, cream cheese, and yogurt in the bowl of a stand mixer, and stir to blend until it is smooth and creamy, about 2 minutes. Keep covered in the refrigerator up to 1 week, but bring it to room temperature before serving or it may be too firm to dip.

TIP! *This dip works well with almost any of the cookie dough flavors.*

Pecan Sandie Cookie Dough Nut Log

Nut logs, like cheese balls and fruitcakes, are due for a comeback. This nut log combines a midcentury modern aesthetic with a cookie dough twist that could easily make it grace the pages of *Dwell* magazine.

1 cup Pecan Sandie Cookie Dough
  (page 20)
1 ½ cups granulated sugar
1 teaspoon salt
1 tablespoon freshly squeezed lemon juice
½ teaspoon baking soda
1 ½ cups roasted, salted nuts
  (pecans, cashews, or peanuts—
  whatever you like)

Wrap the cookie dough in plastic wrap and form a log, about 1 ½ inches in diameter. If the dough is too soft to unwrap and keep its log shape, refrigerate for about 10 minutes to firm.

In a heavy-bottomed pot, heat the sugar, ¼ cup of water, salt, and lemon juice until the sugar melts. Heat the syrup to 310°F. Then remove the syrup from the heat, and add the baking soda. Whisk together to keep the baking soda from clumping. Add the nuts, all at once, and stir to coat. Then spread out the nuts (careful, they'll be hot!) on a parchment-lined baking sheet to cool. When they have cooled completely and hardened, chop about half the brittle into small pieces.

Unwrap the dough, spritz it with a bit of water, and roll in the brittle, evenly coating the whole log. Rewrap the now nut-covered log, and chill for another 15 minutes, just until firm. Serve immediately with the remaining brittle broken into shards.

TIP! *Cashew Caramel Cookie Dough (page 18) would also make an excellent nut log filling.*

Chocolate Hazelnut Cookie Dough Profiteroles

If the choux fits—and oh-my-how-does-it-ever when it's filled with chocolate hazelnut cookie dough smashed ice cream.

MAKES ABOUT 25 PROFITEROLES

1 cup milk
6 tablespoons unsalted butter, melted
1 cup all-purpose flour
2 teaspoons granulated sugar
Pinch of salt
4 large eggs, at room temperature
½ cup Chocolate Hazelnut Cookie Dough (page 17)
1 cup good-quality vanilla ice cream
Chocolate sauce, for drizzling

Preheat the oven to 425°F. Line 2 baking sheets with parchment paper.

In a heavy-bottomed pot over medium heat, combine the milk, butter, flour, sugar, and salt. Stir with a spoon until the mixture thickens and forms into a paste. Continue to cook, stirring constantly, or until the paste dries slightly and a film appears on the sides and bottom of the pot.

Transfer the paste to a stand mixer, and stir at medium speed for 4 minutes, to cool. Increase the speed of the mixer to medium-high, and add the eggs, one at a time, until completely incorporated. The mixture will become smooth and a little bit shiny. If not, add another egg white.

Using a 1½-inch ice-cream scoop (or 2 spoons), drop mounds of the batter onto the parchment, leaving 2 inches between each drop. Smooth out any points with a moistened finger.

Bake at 425°F for 10 minutes. Reduce the heat to 350°F and bake for another 10 minutes, or until golden brown, turning the baking sheet after about 5 minutes. Turn off the oven and let the puffs sit in the cooling oven for about 10 minutes. Remove them from the oven and let cool completely. You can store them in an airtight container for a few days. If they soften, crisp them in the oven at 350°F for a few minutes, and they'll be like new.

When you are ready to serve, slice the cooled puffs in half with a serrated knife.

In a medium bowl, smash the cookie dough into the ice cream. Chill for about 20 minutes if it gets too messy. Sandwich a heaping tablespoon–size scoop of cookie dough ice-cream mixture between the 2 halves, and then drizzle with chocolate sauce. Serve immediately.

FORMULAS for METRIC CONVERSION

OUNCES to GRAMS	multiply ounces by 28.35
POUNDS to GRAMS	multiply pounds by 453.5
CUPS to LITERS	multiply cups by .24
FAHRENHEIT to CENTIGRADE	subtract 32 from Fahrenheit, multiply by 5 and divide by 9

METRIC EQUIVALENTS FOR VOLUME

U.S.	Metric
⅛ tsp.	0.6 ml
¼ tsp.	1.2 ml
½ tsp.	2.5 ml
¾ tsp.	3.7 ml
1 tsp.	5 ml
1½ tsp.	7.4 ml
2 tsp.	10 ml
1 Tbsp.	15 ml
1½ Tbsp.	22.0 ml
2 Tbsp. (⅛ cup/1 fl. oz)	30 ml
3 Tbsp.	45 ml
¼ cup (2 fl. oz)	59 ml
⅓ cup	79 ml
½ cup (4 fl. oz)	118 ml
⅔ cup	158 ml
¾ cup (6 fl. oz)	178 ml
1 cup (8 fl. oz)	237 ml
1¼ cups	300 ml
1½ cups	355 ml
1¾ cups	425 ml
2 cups (1 pint/16 fl. oz)	500 ml
3 cups	725 ml
4 cups (1 quart/32 fl. oz)	.95 liters
16 cups (1 gallon/128 fl. oz)	3.8 liters

OVEN TEMPERATURES

Degrees Fahrenheit	Degrees Centigrade	British Gas Marks
200°	93°	—
250°	120°	½
275°	140°	1
300°	150°	2
325°	165°	3
350°	175°	4
375°	190°	5
400°	200°	6
450°	230°	8

METRIC EQUIVALENTS FOR WEIGHT

U.S.	Metric
1 oz	28 g
2 oz	57 g
3 oz	85 g
4 oz	113 g
5 oz	142 g
6 oz	170 g
7 oz	198 g
8 oz	227 g
16 oz (1 lb.)	454 g
2.2 lbs.	1 kilogram

METRIC EQUIVALENTS FOR BUTTER

U.S.	Metric
2 tsp.	10 g
1 Tbsp.	15 g
1½ Tbsp.	22.5 g
2 Tbsp. (1 oz)	27 g
3 Tbsp.	42 g
4 Tbsp.	56 g
4 oz. (1 stick)	110 g
8 oz. (2 sticks)	220 g

METRIC EQUIVALENTS FOR LENGTH

U.S.	Metric
¼ inch	.65 cm
½ inch	1.25 cm
1 inch	2.50 cm
2 inches	5.00 cm
3 inches	6.00 cm
4 inches	8.00 cm
5 inches	11.00 cm
6 inches	15.00 cm
7 inches	18.00 cm
8 inches	20.00 cm
9 inches	23.00 cm
12 inches	30.50 cm
15 inches	38.00 cm

ACKNOWLEDGMENTS

It takes many cooks to make a cookbook. This one would not have been possible without Holly Schmidt, who piqued my interest with a subject I had no idea how much I'd enjoy; Jordana Tusman, who stuck with the idea even after a few hiccups along the way; Susan Roxborough, who graciously allowed me to take on the project despite an already busy schedule; Carolyn Sobczak, who made the editing process a breeze; Ashley Haag, for a beautiful design; Shannon Wilson, for her excellent recipe testing; and my husband, Cameron, for letting me take over our weekends and evenings to work through the recipes. Thank you all so much for your amazing support!

INDEX

Note: Page references in *italics* indicate photographs.